MindSHIFT into Success:

Seven Things You Can Do to Live a Better Life Starting Now

Cathy J. Herring

www.mindshiftintosuccess.com

MindSHIFT into Success: Seven Things You Can Do to Live a Better Life Starting Now

Cathy J. Herring

Cathy J. Herring

You are invited to please visit my website to receive free resources and join my FREE email list.

https://cathyherring.com

Why Read This Book

There is a SIMPLE way to move out of MISERY and into SUCCESS.

It begins by discovering your best solutions for living your life. This book gives you simple solutions you can start using today.

In this book, you will:

Learn how to move out of MISERY and into success with simple strategies that you can begin today.

Learn how to increase your self-esteem and confidence in a matter of days and be your authentic self.

You too can be the winner you always dreamed of being.

And so much more!

"THE MAGIC BEGINS WITH THESE SIMPLE SOLUTIONS."

What Are Others Saying about This Book?

If you are feeling stuck in your life, MindSHIFT into Success is an inspiring read with easy essential concepts to follow. Cathy's solution approach, "The magic begins with these simple solutions," has a snowball effect. As you move through the chapters and adopt the strategies, you will find yourself experiencing an acceleration of your growth. Cathy's compassionate writing style and real-life experiences give you the tools to make the changes that will lead you to a better life!

Medea Shaw, founder of Daily Happy Up

I'm really enjoying working on your book. Not only this, but I love the way you give all the details for the meditations—very encouraging for your readers :) I'm really enjoying your book.

Ita de Groot, editor

Acknowledgements:

Editor - Ita de Groot

Cover Design -Rebeca Covers

In Loving Memory of

My cherished and forever friend

Erin Patricia Saunders

I loved how you loved life and kept the faith.

May your courageous spirit encourage others.

May your dreams be realized.

You inspired me.

"I AM Light
Health is Wealth
Freedom is essential."

By Erin Saunders

About the Author

Cathy J. Herring, MS, is a licensed professional counselor, a certified life coach, a certified professional hypnotist, an author, and a HeartCore leadership HCL9 graduate with over twenty years of experience in the emotional wellness business. She holds a master's degree in behavioral science. Cathy's personal coaching expertise helps people transform their lives into joyful, happy, and successful ones. She has successfully worked with children, adolescents, adults, couples, and families. She is passionate about helping others improve their mindsets & lifestyles while assisting them discover positive solutions that work for them.

Cathy has witnessed how simple yet effective tools, when implemented, changed her life and the lives of many people she worked with. She wrote this book to share those answers with you.

Besides writing, Cathy runs an online business where she continues to help people navigate emotional gaps and transform them. She loves being outdoors, walking in the woods or on a beach. She enjoys hanging out with her family and meeting up with friends.

For free resources and more information about Cathy Herring and any upcoming workshops, training, retreats, or other current news, please visit her website at www.mindshiftforsuccess.com or www.cathyherring.com Please sign up to receive your free inspiring e-book and join her free fabulous email list where you receive free heart-warming affirmations to keep you inspired.

.

Table of Contents

Chapter 1

Jump on the Bandwagon—The time is now!

Most people only dream about being successful.

Just like it was yesterday, I remembered that day clearly. The crisp, clear blue sky radiated with a bold, bright sun. There was a calm, gentle breeze in the air, and the weather was absolutely perfect. At that precise moment, everything was stunningly quiet and very pristine. I felt like I was in the middle of nowhere. And as we strolled around the trees, there she stood, majestically breathtaking and gleaming with pride. I was awestruck. On the first day of my first trip out of my country, here I am, practically standing underneath Paris's pride and joy—the Eiffel Tower. Seeing her close to us was such a surprise. That moment in time, the perfect day, two weary travelers going for a stroll on our first day in Paris and finding ourselves outside the bustling of the Eiffel Tower as if no other souls were around, was a serene, magical moment.

Have you ever wondered about the facets of living your life?

What if living your life could be different, happier, or easier? Do you often dream of being or doing something new, whether it be empowering your life, finding the love of your life, or being a better parent? You may have realized you want to improve relationships and connections with others, land a new career or create a more aligned lifestyle. Do you feel stuck and want to get off the hamster wheel? If yes, you have come to the right place.

Years before my Paris trip, I realized my lifestyle was not resonating with me. Without further detail, I felt I had been selected for the wrong play. I felt stuck. What about you? Do you ever feel stuck or have difficulty facing life's challenges? Maybe your life isn't what you thought it would be. When I recognized I wasn't living my best life, I realized I needed a new playbook and tools. I began to seek and act.

Inspirational coaches like Louise Hay and Wayne Dyer didn't always feel good about their lives. They knew there was another way, something yet to appear. They found similar solutions that, when applied, improved their lives tremendously. They and other inspirational thought leaders such as Norman Vincent Peale, and Dale Carnegie inspired me. This book is for people who yearn for more. It shares resourceful solutions to help you set cornerstones in your life. These solutions will inspire and enrich people, providing innovative tools for challenging times. Since people are not alike, you may find that some of these solutions work better than others. So, you may prefer some over others. And that's okay. I've found that some people may implement all or just one or two of them. However, these answers are similar, and they can overlap. Usually, most people work on a few methods and add others later to their daily or weekly routines as they become more familiar.

Overall, consistently applying these solutions provides diverse transformations for many folks. For example, some people have found their lives transformed as their confidence and self-esteem improved immediately. Many experts have shared similar stories about their clients increasing their abundance, positive health, mental outlook, prosperity, and thriving lifestyles by applying similar positive strategies. These methods are my go-to's for myself and others because, with implementation, they have shown they work to improve people's lives. These solutions help you thrive so you can enjoy more options in your life.

So, I ask you, what are you longing for? Wouldn't it be exciting to experience profound relationships with others or reach for that new career you've been dreaming of? Wouldn't it be encouraging to feel more confident, self-assured, and make decisions more quickly? This book's solutions may start a new lease on your life with your friends and loved ones. What are you waiting for? Maybe you want an improved way of living and being. That is a great idea! Think about this question: How much more time do you have left on your life's calendar?

The time is now.

This book intends to help the many people who are ready to be more successful with their businesses, relationships, and living life. People who want positive changes, especially busy people who believe they are too busy to apply the needed strategies. People who feel stuck and are ready to overcome challenges will find solutions in this book too. This book shares easy-to-apply, ordinary life solutions that work to improve your life beginning now.

For some people making a slight shift in perception or action can bring immediate rewards—just like magic. The core idea introduces you to seven notions and shares how they are already effective in people's lives. This book explains how to apply each concept and the possible outcomes. This book intends to help you quickly confront life's challenges by creating resourceful tools to utilize daily. Truly joyful, happy people have resources available to help them overcome and walk through life's challenges. This book's intention is to teach you many of the same tools that truly joyful people live by. It's best to begin with an open mind as you implement these strategies. Then with trial and error, revise if needed.

Working with many others wanting improvement in their lives in one way or another has helped me understand there are a few secrets that, when consistently applied, can dramatically improve your life immediately. I have witnessed these results time and time again through the eyes of my clients. Here are some of the results people have shared with me after applying these simple solutions: Overcoming the negative repercussions of life so that they experience increased happiness, self-assurance, joy, courage, and an improved mental outlook. I have utilized these solutions with adolescents, married couples, college students, and adults. I have seen some people experience a complete change overnight, and many demonstrate lifelong positive changes over time. These tools have shown immediate relief and long-term growth for many customers. And as I have seen, with consistent utilization, there may be more growth over time. Some have even shared that they experienced a positive "mind shift." As you read through this book, I encourage you not to underestimate the power of these simple life solutions. Take what works and resonates with you and leave the rest.

In this book, I share stories and simple methods people have utilized to change their lives positively. They have shared that they have experienced many positive changes, such as increased happiness, self-assurance, joy, courage, and an improved mental outlook. I have utilized these solutions with adolescents, married couples, college students, and adults. I have seen some people experience a complete perceptional change overnight, and others demonstrate lifelong positive changes over time. Overall, implanting these tools has helped some immediately relieve their present dilemma. With consistent utilization there, the potential is higher for more positive changes. Many folks experience a complete positive "Mind*shift*"—an improved way of living.

Going to Paris, France, opened new insights and possibilities. My experience may not be something you wish to do, but I told you my story to demonstrate the power of the positive changes I experienced using the tools I discuss in this book. Years earlier,

I had recognized that my adult life was not resonating with my values and wishes. I was not living an experience that resonated with me. There was so much more. I yearned for a better career, improved relationships, spiritual connectedness, and a more fulfilling life, true to my soul purpose, for my children and myself. I began my journey by increasing my awareness and applying positive new perspectives.

Some people I've worked with experience negative limiting beliefs. They habitually self-criticize or blame their circumstances on others. As was the case with Philip. He shared with me that he was unhappy with his life and felt his current poor marriage was the result of his wife's actions, not his. Even though I have no idea if what he shares with me is truthful, I take him at his word. I assess more about him as I give him feedback and listen to his reply. Whether or not what he tells me is true is irrelevant. He believes his story is truthful. He thinks his misery stems from other people's actions.

Instead of confronting his beliefs, I suggest he use a strategy to enlighten his awareness. I explain, "Whether or not these people are making you miserable, you are the only one seeking help, and you are the only one you can change."

He nodded his head as if he understood. Now he feels validated and is not as resistant to being open to something new. I ask him if he's ready for something different. As he shrugs his shoulders, Philip admits he's tired of how he lives, doesn't want to lose his wife, and is ready to try something different. "Great," I reply. "You are in the right place."

After sharing two different approaches, he chooses one to start his journey. We work on the technique in the session. He quickly learned and left with a new tool to utilize until he returned for his next session.

I resonated with many of you when I set about improving my circumstances. I needed clarification on what I needed. My priority began with searching for a better-paying and more satisfying career so I could successfully support my children and myself. I finished my bachelor's degree and quickly obtained my master's. After earning my degree, I became more experienced in counseling. As I worked with clients, I immediately noticed their positive changes. Some people were experiencing increased self-awareness, self-image, and confidence, especially women. Their positive results never ceased to amaze me.

As I continued to study and work with others, I began applying some of these methods to my own life. I noticed experiencing positive growth immediately. I realized as I reached one plateau, new ones would open. Sometimes my endeavors were more complex and took longer than anticipated. Many times, I would find myself "stuck in a rut." Regardless, I continued to persevere. Living life successfully, as I discovered, is a lifelong process.

Successful people are resilient. They know how to go the distance. You will never stop facing obstacles in your life. To succeed and maintain that you must learn how to overcome those obstacles like successful people do.

Successful people have strategies in place. They have built up their resilience. The techniques in this book can similarly assist you. They can be your cornerstone core foundational strategies, which, when implemented, will help you build your resilience. As stated earlier, living a happy and contented life involves an open mind, ownership of your life, and incorporating lifelong learning, growing, and changing.

When Philip returned the following week, I saw a significant change in his demeanor and heard a more confident attitude. It was apparent he was already experiencing improvements from doing and applying his homework. It was as if a lightbulb had come on. Now, he seemed hopeful and had a gleam in his eyes. He happily shared he felt better and was excited to continue. Over the next six months, his shift was terrific as he continued to work with me, applying many of the things I shared in this book. Eventually, he took ownership of his actions and personal outcome. He claimed he was more content with his life, and his marriage had improved significantly. He shared he was beginning to feel happy again.

Thus, I earned my master's degree in behavioral counseling in 1999. I have been a licensed professional counselor and licensed alcohol and drug counselor for over twenty years. I now have extensive training, experience, and certifications in other mental health and life coaching approaches, such as hypnosis, NLP, EMDR basic, and life coaching. I coach customers to overcome stuck thought patterns, reach their goals, or improve their lives with group life coaching or individual hypnosis and life coaching at https://cathyherring.com

As of this writing, I have worked in the mindset-shifting business for over twenty years, and these methods have assisted hundreds in gaining a newfound perspective. I am very passionate about what I do. Here are some of the significant results my clients have experienced when applying these strategies while working with me:

- Increased self-awareness
- Improved relationships
- Less judgmental and blaming
- Increased contentment
- Increased confidence and clarity
- Increased peace, serenity, and assuredness
- More joyful
- Less stressed
- Improved family interactions
- More courageous and adventurous
- Upleveling their career
- Better decision-making skills
- Dragon slayers (or at least they felt like one!)

Suppose you want to improve your relationships, find the love of your life, get that extraordinary career, be a good parent, or whatever you want to strive for. In that case, you can reach more successful outcomes as you aim for your goals with these simplified strategies. People who have consistently applied these principles to their lives have experienced many successes in many of their endeavors.

Living a satisfying and enriching life is a process; learning new solutions is a process. Implementing strategies and seeing excellent results is a process too. However, please keep reading if you are ready for an inner personal transformation, a refreshing attitude, more confidence and courage, and improved relationships and lifestyle. You may find yourself with a new lease on life with your friends and loved ones. You may find yourself more confident, self-assured, and making decisions more quickly. What if you changed your career or found the love of your life? Applying these strategies can help you live an improved lifestyle, no matter what success means to you.

Thus, this was the first time I had ventured out of the USA, and I had never imagined it was possible. Just like magic, there I was in Paris. I was living a dream I had never had earlier in my lifetime. Therefore, when I changed, my life changed.

I am excited you are taking your first step by reading this book. Are you ready to better yourself? Keep on reading. As you read on and apply some of these methods, some of your thoughts about what is most important in your life will likely change. Be thinking about how success would look for you. Imagine what your life will be like when you are successful.

Best wishes for a successful journey.

Chapter 2

What Is Stopping You?

Have you ever reminisced and thought, "Gee, if only I had known that I wouldn't have missed those opportunities!" Of course, everyone has at some time or another. Unfortunately, we cannot redo the past or live in the past. It would be best to recognize and seize opportunities as they arise in your life, today and not yesterday. One of this book's intentions is to prepare you not to live in the past and be ready now.

From time to time, my client, Maude, shared that she was stuck in the past. As she gained more clarity and confidence with her mental, physical, and spiritual healing, I noticed that the memories of past events and stuck situations had an uncanny way of just bubbling up to the surface. She shared with me many times how different opportunities had passed her by and what she thought she might have missed out on if she had acted differently. She told me she was closer to promising opportunities than she really knew. Of course, she didn't know what they would have been, but she thought some of her earlier decisions would have been different from what she knows now.

One day she said she realized she was conditioned to live small, and anything outside her space seemed huge. I remembered how she was comparing the mentality of her younger years as if she were like a fish swimming in a fishbowl. As she looked off into the wild blue yonder, Maude shared she felt like she was inside the bowl and could clearly see those living outside the glass bowl, but she never saw herself as one of those people. "I was longing, but I felt I was not worthy enough," she loudly reminisced.

Maude's story reminded me of my own. When I was much younger, we still got our books at the bookstores, and Amazon and the Internet were up and coming; I was drawn to self-help books, such as those by Norman Vincent Peale, Dale Carnegie, Wayne Dyer, and even Tony Robbins' first book. These authors would share their personal stories and would often give suggestions on how to be more assertive, confident, and self-assured, overcome fear, and accomplish something fantastic, like speaking in front of enormous audiences. Their books and stories taught me there were different ways of living life. I loved reading their stories about how they overcame something and were now living their dream lives. Even though I believed in their outcomes, I had difficulty relating their message to my life situation.

Reflecting back, in my soul, there was something amiss. I sensed a vague and empty void, but I couldn't yet see or name it. However, my soul knew, and I believe that's why I was drawn to these inspiring and motivating books. But I don't remember making the connections that I could expand my mindset and live my life fuller. I read about these authors as if they lived in another world, in another dimension. I didn't see myself doing what they even suggested. I was shy and apprehensive that I would obtain similar results.

Looking back at those earlier years, here I was in my earliest adult years with answers and solutions for my soul's calling in my hands, but I wasn't ready. I didn't have clarity. At least, that's what my mind told me. This happened to those people but not to me. I couldn't possibly do what they were doing. I lived through their stories and achievements. I knew there was something much bigger than me. Their stories inspired me. Their books seemed to jump out at me at the bookstores, but I wasn't getting the message! Deep down inside, I didn't believe I was good enough, so why bother? Regardless of my decision or indecision, time continued on.

Think about this: Every New Year, highly motivated and inspired people like you write out astounding resolutions they're committed to achieving. Many have excellent intentions and start their journeys.

Yet before January ends, research shows many have abandoned pursuing those fantastic goals. Why is that? Have you been guilty of doing so? Have you attempted to achieve something and stopped before reaching the goal? If so, what do you think your "reason" was? What will your reason be for not taking action here?

Maybe you're too busy. Perhaps you don't think you'll get the results you want. Maybe you'll put them off until next week or next month. Perhaps you think you're comfortable with your life after all. Do you think this way of living is just easier? Maybe you don't like change.

The change will happen regardless. Perhaps the problem is someone else's fault. I wonder if you feel apprehensive, unworthy, fearful, or not good enough deep down inside. What will hold you back?

Your body, mind, and spiritual being are designed beautifully to assist you with always maintaining your health and safety. For instance, if you have a "fear of change," you will more likely find other things to keep you occupied than seeking transformational change. Some people do this simply by complaining enough until they have successfully talked themselves out of taking the chance. Others who don't feel good enough about themselves will hesitate because subconsciously, they may be thinking, *Why*

11

would I pursue something I don't think I can obtain? Many people, yourself included, don't finish what they started for many reasons. Some are legitimate, but most are experiencing stuck thoughts or resistance.

Basically, this is how survival works for many of us. From ages 0 to 7, we are in our developmental years. Without remembering most of these formative years, you developed and created some of your most significant ideas, thoughts, values, and perceptions about operating within your social construct. During this time, you were also modeling and adopting many beliefs, actions, and feelings of those around you. And before you blame your parents, research has shown some situations, on any given day, may have unintentionally shaped something negatively for you without your caregivers or parents even knowing.

Even with the best intentions, life events happen during our formative years. Regardless, your parents or caregivers did their best with what they knew at the time. With that said, you have some built-in survival thinking you are probably unaware of. Some have been formed to keep you safe, which may no longer be needed. Also, as you live your life, you can create more permanent thoughts, basically formed to keep you from suffering in one way or another, including resistant thinking. That doesn't mean these thoughts are logical or pertain to your current situation, but they can still be activated from time to time, again and again. However, this doesn't mean you must keep them and remain stuck in whatever pursuit you are attempting to reach. If you have some of those survival thoughts, don't panic. Most of us, upon inner inspections, will find some, especially resistance thinking. But if you're seeking a lifestyle change, some old styles need to be addressed.

I'm not telling you this information to keep you stuck or handing you a defense to let you continue using these excuses. That decision is yours to make because there is good news. Research has also demonstrated that you will continue to grow, learn, and change throughout your life. We can change our thinking process. We can change our thoughts. For instance, all the motivational influencers I previously mentioned did confront their resistant thinking. Doing so helped them rise to be the people they were meant to be and live the life they were meant to live. Knowing this information will help you confront your resistance and rise beyond this matter. Hence the word "*mind-shift.*"

The following is a sampling of popular underlying themes of some common stuck/resistant thoughts you or others may be experiencing. To help clarify how these thoughts work, some of the personal excuses for each follow:

1. I'm not good enough. (Why even try or attempt? Those people are better than me.)

2. I don't deserve this. (I can't achieve this goal because it's out of my reach. Again, keeping you safe by not changing anything.)

3. What if something "bad" happens? (Projecting fear onto the situation so doing nothing keeps you safe.)

4. I don't have the time. (This is not important enough. This can be an avoidance technique, also.)

5. What will others think? (This phrase keeps you from being accountable to yourself and your needs.)

6. I can't do this. (This resists the unknown. This is avoiding being apprehensive or fearful. If you do not attempt, you will not fail.)

7. She's got the looks, smartness, money, or whatever else. (Justify why you can't achieve that goal. You are shortchanged; it's not your fault.)

Do any of these sound familiar to you? Can you see how difficult it would be to be open to change if these thoughts unconsciously challenge you? If none of those resonated with you, find some others that you tell yourself often or that you hear your parents telling you. The resistant or stuck thoughts are real in the person's mind who is self-rehearsing them.

As these statements rummage in their minds repeatedly, they persuade their owners—people like you—that they are true and genuine. This type of thinking is one of the reasons people are not able to fully live their lives.

Think about this: If these same or similar thoughts keep playing in your head and nothing else changes, you get the same results. Our minds believe those thoughts are true! Thus, how challenging would it be for you if you've already convinced yourself they're true? So if you are experiencing anything similar, this may be why you're not successfully achieving your life goals. You will likely need to confront and overcome any resistant thought patterns that keep you stuck. Throughout this book, you will learn and have many opportunities to apply new skills to challenge and help you replace your resistant thinking.

Maude's story demonstrates how her resistant thinking messed with her mind and kept her stuck for years. In one of our phone meetups, Maude confided in me and laid all her negative beliefs on the table. She shared she had difficulty reaching her goals because she recognized she didn't deserve better. And then, when Maude didn't achieve her milestone, she shared she would berate herself even more. Even though she realized not reaching those goals was common for many people. She wanted to be different.

One day, after sharing her frustrations and dreams with me again, the lightbulb came on. She realized she was tired of discussing her frustrations and lack of action. She was ready to experience her breakthrough. She immediately began applying more concepts and diligently working through them. Maude started to work through her resistance by journaling more and more. She journaled about her gratefulness in her *Attitude of Gratitude* journal. She journaled about her negative self-concepts and reframed her thinking into empowering affirmations. Those solutions became her homework assignments. Over the next few weeks, she constantly applied herself as we worked toward setting more attainable goals based on her needs, wishes, and timeline. She was on fire; she seemed to be soaring and reaching several milestones. Then bam! It was as if she had hit a brick wall head-on. Suddenly, she began questioning herself again. Then she shut down.

Can you relate to any of this? Do you stop when you are making headway? Do you have stories you tell yourself? Do you wonder why you do not reach your goals? Do you procrastinate even when necessary action is dear to your heart? Do you find yourself putting things off for later, but later never arrives? Do you entertain thoughts like *I'm not important* or *I don't really need that anyway?* You get the picture.

Norman Vincent Peale wrote a book titled *You Can If You Think You Can.* And I say this is true too; "If nothing changes, nothing changes." You must add changes if you're not living your authentic life and reaching your goals. Which path will you choose?

We all experience resistance from time to time. You are not alone. You and others like you are the reason I want to share this message. Experiencing resistance or justifying excuses not to accomplish your goals or not living the life you want to live is easy. Putting things off until tomorrow, which never comes, seems easier than achieving our goals. Do you like putting those tasks off? Not really, and you don't need to continue to live like that.

I continued meeting up with Maude, but she seemed listless. She claimed she was still working on her assignments but had lost her enthusiasm. One day she admitted she was paralyzed with fear. She knew her pesky little thoughts had invaded again. She was highly disappointed in her progress and wondered why she backtracked. I reminded her this was normal, and all was well.

15

As you progress, you are peeling off layers of your onion, one by one. Usually, new layers of junk appear, and you need to confront those too. The layers shrink as you continue to peel back, and eventually, you easily handle what's left because you have new tools. I identified Maude's strengths and reminded her how much progress she had made. Maude admitted she was not taking action like she did before. We worked on a mindfulness meditation before she left. She was instructed to apply the meditation daily. She agreed she would.

This book has solutions for you. Successful people live with specific concepts that serve as guideposts for them. These beliefs serve as their foundational moral compass, assisting them in living their best life. Those notions can also help a person stay focused and accomplish their goals. If valid for them, these can also work for you. These are simple. You may not have thought of living with some of these concepts. However, these solutions work for many people.

Some of you may wonder if you'll have time to implement some of these concepts. Yes, many people incorporate these into their everyday living, and more than likely, these solutions will become part of your daily living, too. Once you learn these, you can seamlessly integrate them as part of your everyday living. Many of you are asking yourself if these solutions will benefit you at your age. Absolutely! There is no age limit to this. You can benefit from implementing these concepts when you experience self-doubt, low self-worth, anxious symptoms, stress overload, relationship conflicts, not reaching goals, or encountering resistance. Your age does not matter.

Maybe you're asking yourself, *If these are so simple, why aren't most people already utilizing them?* Some people use them, and without thinking, they return to their old familiar patterns. Some people haven't grasped how beneficial this is, so they don't even try. Others don't know. Many may return to old habits if they're not pre-prepared, especially during a crisis.

Once again, do you wonder if living your life could be more abundant, prosperous, or joyful? Do you implement new goals, then wane? Do you often dream of reaching a new plateau, changing careers, earning higher wages, having improved relationships, experiencing a great marriage, or being a better parent? Reaching those wishes begins with getting yourself ready with healthy, supportive tools.

When Maude and I met again, she was a bit better but not entirely on track. She still seemed scared to move forward. She began pouring out more negative beliefs to me. I heard some standard themes, like "I can't do this" and "I don't deserve this." She was hesitant to move forward; she wasn't sure of herself. She admitted she realized she felt like an imposter. Maude had shared that she thought she was doing excellent work, but now she can't. I nodded and gently reminded her that, from time to time, these roadblocks would appear. The fear of doubt had raised its ugly head and again created resistance. I've seen this phenomenon occur again and again. I reassured Maude she is doing a great job and there was hope. "Let's build on your progress and take you back before the decline." She agreed she would do that. She worked on reframing her thoughts into positive ones and added an empowerment meditation before leaving.

Applying these concepts can be the beginning of a new journey for you! Wouldn't it be exciting to improve your relationships with others or reach for that new career? Wouldn't it be more thrilling to feel more confident, self-assured, and make decisions more quickly? Absolutely! You and what's inside of you are at the heart of the matter. Everything in your life revolves around you. Remember, you have this powerful hidden potential waiting to be unleashed. Applying these concepts can help you tap into your inner being and unleash your powerful innate potential.

I'm happy to report that Maude stayed on her path, with a few bumps here and there; her confidence and well-being soared as she practiced applying her concepts and completing her goals.

Her courage and confidence increased, and more positive opportunities began opening up for her. With the theories as her guiding post, she climbed out of fear and expanded her perception. Then she began living a more satisfying and authentic lifestyle. It was a miracle watching Maude change her life and live the life she deserved. I was happy for her.

So, what about you? Do you ever feel like you're standing on the shoreline, wanting to get to the other side? This book intends to provide a bridge for you to cross over. You can enhance your life also. Why wait any longer? Let's get started.

Chapter 3

The 7 Essential Concepts

Upon returning from stepping out to get a cup of coffee, my next client was waiting for me. His pitch-black, sleek, shiny hair greeted me when I entered my office. He sat with his head hanging down, barely responding as I greeted him. I noticed he seemed nervous as he wrung his hands back and forth. I wondered what had happened since I saw him last week. Enrico was a shy college student but was usually bubbly and upbeat during his visits.

As I sat down, I sighed. I asked Enrico to take a deep breath and let it out slowly with a huge sigh. Upon doing so, I could see some instant relief. When I inquired with my usual "How is it going?" He tensed up again and barely whispered that he was flunking college.

Surprised and taken aback, I asked, "How so?"

He just shook his head at me. After five or ten minutes, he finally whispered that he didn't know why.

"What?" I gently inquired with a concerned look. "That doesn't sound like you. Please tell me what is happening?"

"I know the material, but I can't pass the tests. I freeze and don't remember," he stammered. "I'm going to flunk my classes!"

"Oh, so you know the material but can't pass the tests," I resonated with him. "I see."

Sitting there with Enrico, I pondered what would be the best approach for his situation. He sighed as he continued with his story.

As I listened, I reassured him. "The Enrico I know is smart, caring, honest, and witty. I have no reason not to believe you can't study and pass those tests."

He perked up, engaged in eye contact, and was eager to listen to what I was about to share with him.

There are several methods in these concepts people have greatly benefited from, such as helping empower them and addressing the situation at hand. Working with different clients and seeing their results, these approaches or combinations have assisted hundreds of people in enhancing their abilities for success with various endeavors. Utilizing these concepts gives you the tools to be proactive in your endeavors, even without emotional challenges.

Let's review the seven essential concepts that we will examine in the chapters to come:

1.   The Attitude of Gratitude

The Attitude of Gratitude concept encourages one to focus on what they have and what works well in their life. This concept is an important technique to help one focus on what is working for them rather than what is not. When one does so, their focus returns to the haves instead of the have-nots. Time and time again, when people stress out over what's not going right for them, they forget to think about what they do have, no matter how small it may be. Doing so can help people maintain an optimistic attitude and outlook even during stressful times.

Refocusing your mindset by concentrating on positive effects enhances people's well-being by providing a refreshing, encouraging perspective.

Being thankful focuses on what a person already has and can be ongoing and endless. You may think of your characteristics, family and friends, employment, school, faith, affiliated support group, other situations, material things, valuables, finances, and food. Anything that is an asset for you, whether you like it or not. Overall, this concept helps remind you of what you have and what is currently working for you, no matter how small your list may be.

Giving thanks and being grateful daily is a spiritual blessing for your optimum well-being. You send healthy vibrational energy into the universe every time you give thanks for your gifts. Spiritually, this energy can return these healthy vibes to your life. Thus, you may receive many blessings by giving thanks and having an attitude of gratitude.

2. Affirmations and Slogans

Slogans and affirmations are slightly different, but their features blend well together, so I usually discuss them simultaneously. Affirmations help a person be positive and change their perception. They can be motivating, inspiring, and desired statements of something you want to achieve or reach. This concept helps you get beyond limiting mind beliefs, also known as "stuck points."

Slogans assist you with addressing a sensitive issue or issues on the spot. They're easy to memorize, and help redirect your thinking, so you don't get unfocused. The overall goal is to stay emotionally detached so you can address a particular challenge for yourself and keep yourself moving in a positive direction.

These techniques can help you retrain your thoughts to overcome resistance, limiting beliefs, or negative perceptions. They're also useful as quick reference tools helping you maintain

21

vibrant energy and a mindful attitude. Researchers link being successful to being dependent on your perception. Keeping a few of these positive statements handy to easily access and retrain your thinking helps you maintain your best thinking.

3. Positive Thinking – Reframing Your Negative Thinking

The positive self-talk technique helps retrain your thoughts so you think more positively and communicate optimistically. This concept enables you to identify negative self-talk messages and replace them with better options. This method is also utilized to challenge self-messages such as fear, worry, and doubt. It would be best if you embraced thinking positively about living your life successfully more often than not.

Articulating clear and concise information is a robust, healthy attribute. Clear communication is essential for experiencing healthy relationships within all life's faucets. Be mindful that everyone's perceptions differ depending on their understanding of the message. Our interpretations depend on our perception of the knowledge and how concise and clear the message is. However, we may need further explanations due to diverse dialects, communities, and cultural backgrounds.

Research has shown your mind is powerful. Many studies have shown that the thoughts you feed your brain affect how you live. Our thinking can guide our moods and our actions. So how will your thoughts drive your lifestyle? Will the result be what you want? In this book, you will learn how to examine, create, and apply these techniques to experience more happiness, joy, and prosperity.

4. Mindfulness and Meditation

Mindfulness and meditation are excellent resources for calming the mind and regaining clarity. Mindfulness focuses on the present, whereas meditation focuses on a particular outcome. Both are solutions for confronting life's challenges and helping you maintain vibrant energy. Embracing these techniques provides most people with a calm, tranquil state of mind.

Western society has been skeptical about these methods since meditating was associated with particular religions or cults and originated from Eastern cultures. However, people seem to be discovering that utilizing these methods can be very beneficial and practiced to suit their needs or religious expectations. Thus, these methods are becoming increasingly more common in practice. They're easy to learn and don't require much time to apply.

Meditation and mindfulness have several benefits, such as relaxation, increased clarity, courage, self-esteem, and decreased tension and stress. These help improve your calmness, concentration, and emotional balance.

In this book, I'll address the art of breathing in and out appropriately within a relaxed state of mind. I'll explain and provide methods for meditation, including mindfulness, relaxation, and visualization, which I'll introduce you to later in this book.

Practicing meditation can assist you in clearing away mental clutter and recentering yourself. Research has shown that proper meditation significantly benefits your mind and body. Short, consistent meditation is an essential tool for your health and well-being. All these benefits can help you be successful.

5. Nutrition and Daily Movement

Research has shown that a person's eating habits impact their immune system and mental outlook. Healthy ideas, such as adding more healthy options to your food choices, are discussed in this chapter. Feeling well and staying fit are essential for success. Experiencing movement and exercising increases our healthy well-being and provides us with a more positive outlook. In this segment, I focus on two crucial elements of physical well-being, nutrition, and movement.

Daily movement and proper nutrition are two key elements essential for your excellent health. Your body is designed to move and eat healthily. Our best health is valuable to living successfully.

Being mindful of our physical health is important. Good physical health improves one's ability to focus and concentrate. Most people have an aversion to "exercise," so this book refers to exercise as physical movement or daily activities. Since your body was made to move, get up and move it. Walk around the house, do stretches, or follow Pilates or yoga for indoor ideas. There are interesting programs on YouTube, including great ones for the kids that adults could utilize too. For outdoors, simple ones are walking, running, biking, hiking, and swimming, to name a few. Some of you may be interested in joining a gym. The experts say to do some type of vigorous movement for thirty minutes three to four times a week minimum. Good physical movement increases your endorphins which is an excellent source for increasing your positive mood.

6. **Recognizing Your Core Values**

Knowing and understanding your core values is essential. Core values are your beliefs and qualities that guide your thinking and behavior. Your core values impact your thinking and behavior as you navigate your life. At times, your priorities may fluctuate, and so will your values. Many of our values are formed during childhood. People have changed their values, too, as they have changed.

It's important to understand your essential values and see how they help or hinder you. The more your values complement your way of living, the more successful you will be. In a perfect world, you want your core values to align with how you think and act. If they do, great—you're on the right track. If they don't, maybe something needs to be reevaluated. Sometimes friends can be helpful here. For instance, a person wants a better social life, yet they value introversion and quietness, creating opposing desires.

Maybe you desire more spontaneity, yet you value moderation and prudence. This book provides a starting point to see your discrepancies and make minor adjustments.

The crucial point is not to have your most critical values conflict with your essential yearnings. What's an acceptable compromise that you can live with that improves your life if they do conflict? Those answers and an -inclusive list of core values can be found in Chapter 9.

7. Spirituality

Spirituality is the essence of a person's soul and an essential core value. Connecting to your spirituality helps you tune into your sense of purpose, meaning, and wisdom. While there are many more aspects to religion and spirituality than this book mentions, their importance in your life matters whether you're more comfortable in a religious setting or prefer to practice your spirituality more personally. You'll find emotional and even physical benefits in both. A spiritual belief system is integral to personal growth and development and improves mental and physical health. So don't be afraid to explore the deeper truths and what they mean to you.

Typically, spirituality is the inward journey process. Spiritually, a person seeks a personal connection to help one understand oneself and why one does something. Spirituality encourages inner reflection and is often practiced alone. However, many religions encompass a spiritual component within their content. Either or both are important for living a better life. Living spirituality helps you have compassion, understanding, healthy boundaries with others, and a moral compass. Spiritual people tend to experience clarity and focus and lead a relevant life.

Enrico was witty, intelligent, and a quick learner. He was experiencing something real in his life, and he believed that if something didn't change, he wouldn't pass his coursework. A results-driven quick solution is what he needed. So, after a lengthy discussion, I suggested Enrico implement some positive affirmations. He was curious and willing to try anything. I explained how they worked and how he might benefit. Together we created five affirmations he could implement immediately. For his homework, he was to role-play, stating them out loud three times each twice a day while looking at himself in the mirror. He wrote them down. He rehearsed before he left. Then he left. I wouldn't hear from him again for a week.

This book helps you understand that there's a roadmap to help you keep your struggles at a minimum and maximize your successes, no matter how big or small. This book introduces immediate inspirational solutions to empower people. These solutions can help create excellent habits to enable you to maximize your best self. Or, if you don't like routines, you'll be aware of these resources and have them in your toolbox. This book can assist you if you're looking for a renewed sense of accomplishment and satisfaction.

I saw people's pain and struggles as they dealt with personal life challenges, but many of these concepts helped them when they were ready for change and applied them. This book is about people who benefited from using these tools when I worked as their counselor or life coach. Though the names and circumstances have been changed, these situations and results are based on true situations. You may or may not identify with these experiences. However, these tools can be universally applied to diverse situations. You don't need to experience what my clients have experienced to receive beneficial results.

In our fast-paced, hectic world, you'll benefit from the change you can create with these tools. These concepts are quick and easy to learn and apply. Many can be implemented in your daily life without wasting time. The strategies are simple solutions that, when executed, can provide immediate relief, and improve your focus, clarity, satisfaction, and happiness. These solutions increase awareness and provide a strong foundation for living your life and guidance for a more prosperous life.

So, what happened to Enrico? His transformation surprised me. He was ready, and he believed in the remedy. He claimed he began role-playing that evening and continued morning and night. When I saw him a week later, he appeared to be a changed man. He seemed more confident, happy, less anxious, and reassured. His radiant smile appeared as he confidently stated he had passed his first test that week. Enrico continued to work with me for a few months longer. He absorbed the learning, applied it, and got positive results. He was a model client. I was genuinely delighted by his newfound freedom.

Seeing clients like him tremendously benefit is why I wanted to write this book. In the pages ahead, may you also discover what you're looking for—clarity, improved self-esteem, focus, a renewed sense of self, increased joy, engaging conversation with others, improved relationships, more courage, creating a new life and being successful. The magic begins with these simple solutions.

Chapter 4

An Attitude of Gratitude

"Nothing is going right!" sobbed Erika while on a video call with me. "My ex-husband is making me crazy. He's trying to make me look tainted. I don't have time to deal with him between working and caring for the children. What am I going to do?" she distraughtly demanded while sobbing simultaneously.

As I reflected with her on what she had just relayed to me, I had a flash of another mother, Shirley, being in similar shoes and feeling hopeless. At that time, Shirley clearly informed me, "I am their mother first, and I don't understand why their father doesn't understand that!"

As I looked at Erika, I silently heard, "Just let me be their mother," underneath all her frustration and disappointment.

I shared, "Yes, you are their mother first and always will be."

She looked up with pleading eyes and acknowledged what I had just said.

I nodded in agreement as I continued talking. "Everything you're telling me is true, true for you," as I watched her face light up. As I acknowledged, her concerns were validated. I continued, "I know this is tough for you. And I'm not here to minimize what you're saying. Do you understand?"

Now she's looking at me intently and nodding her head up and down.

"What you're experiencing is real, and you cannot change these events at this moment. You and I don't have any control over your ex-husband's actions. Are you with me?"

"Yes," she said with dried-up tears smeared down her face.

"Good," I acknowledged. "You must think about yourself; you are strong," as I gave her a big thumbs up.

She smiled.

"Now, I want you to listen carefully." I continued in my most serious tone; I said, "Do you understand?"

When people present to me in a heightened state of alert, I must quickly assess the situation and decide if they are safe and unhurt. When they are, then my first response is to stabilize them emotionally. I usually do this with an empowerment strategy.

Some of my customers never had a cheerleader on their side. Some have experienced very little faith and belief in themselves. My job is to help empower them so that they can regroup. I want them to advocate for themselves if needed and not be revictimized. People are usually naturally resilient. They may feel emotionally unworthy, fabricating a vicious cycle of self-defeating behaviors. Sometimes when people experience traumatic circumstances, their perspectives become constricted, and they have difficulty being objective and making rational decisions. Remaining in a victim-mentality will only make matters worse for her. Again, returning to her story, I'm not suggesting negative things didn't happen to her. I'm redirecting her to help her squash self-defeating, emotionally charged thoughts from the situation so that she can stabilize herself and begin her self-empowerment. Erika and I will revisit this event once she's emotionally stronger.

After she's stabilized and more open to suggestions, I'll work with Erika with different interchangeable techniques. Most of these methods work simultaneously and will work well for her. People tend to prefer some strategies better than others. That's fine too. Erika and I addressed the Attitude of Gratitude on this day, even though she wasn't feeling too grateful. She owned her worthiness, courage, and tenacity as we worked together.

I suggested an Attitude of Gratitude journal for her. When other clients get involved with the gratitude journal writing, their perspectives and mental clarity immediately improve. When people are experiencing stressful life events, degrading relationships, or negative self-talk, thinking optimistically can be complicated. Validating gratefulness has shown tremendous benefits for anxious, scared, and worried people. Many people have found that this technique provides a calming and self-soothing effect. Customers stated they felt better and more optimistic when using this practice. This technique is easy to apply and provides excellent results. This method works well and quickly for many. I have witnessed significant life-changing transformations as people utilize this journaling technique. Many people experience improved mindsets and higher energy within a few days. This journal can be an excellent tool to keep your attitude in check, especially when unexpected situations arise, much like the one Erika experienced. Plus, this is a healthy tool for fine-tuning your perspectives, keeping you centered and empowered.

However, within my line of work, people who feel downtrodden and anxious tend to forget they have something to be grateful for, especially within the US. Even people doing well are taken aback when I suggest keeping an Attitude of Gratitude journal. For instance, what would you answer if I asked you what you're grateful for, regardless of experiencing positive or negative situations? Most people initially can't think of a thing. I'd probably remind you to pay close attention to what you have and ask questions such as whether you have a roof over your head, something to eat, clothes on your back, and good health.

You might answer, "Well, of course."

Writing those items down and giving thanks for having them empowers people like you.

Perhaps you're on a budget and retort, "I don't like my food, my house is in disarray, and my clothes are hand-me-downs," implying you wish you had more.

I would genuinely inquire, "What would your life be like if you didn't have any of those items you mentioned?"

More than likely, you would tell me, "Even worse."

My point is miracles are created when we mindfully demonstrate our thankfulness. You have something valuable, but you may not be aware of the act of being thankful for what you have. This technique's purpose is to be grateful for what you presently have in your life. This strategy is empowering and one to keep in your tool belt.

Your gratitude journal is a purposeful tool to help you raise awareness of the blessings you already possess. Think of your items as basically anything that makes your life work. If you get stuck, turn this idea around and think, *What would my life be like if I didn't have such and such?* The answer can range from material things, personal characteristics, friends and family, talents, work, and spirituality. You may write down the same thing many times or add variations. It works either way. However, many people have found that variation adds more spontaneity to this exercise while expanding their mindset.

Here are some of the many benefits of doing this journal that I have experienced, have witnessed with my clients, or as noted by research:

1. Thankful people tend to be more grounded and less stressed.

2. People who demonstrate more gratefulness claim they are more optimistic and energetic.

3. Thankful people exhibit higher self-esteem.

4. Empowerment brings clarity, inner strength, and positive engagement.

5. Some state they experience greater awareness and acceptance.

6. Being grateful brings a sense of greater satisfaction, connectedness, and peace.

Overall, one demonstrates more compassion, love, and forgiveness for humankind when they are grateful. They become more optimistic, which has led to being more interactive and supportive within their community. They willingly want to be more involved with living life and helping others. Many are more motivated and inspired to set and reach personal goals and intentions. People who experience gratitude consistently live an enriching and fuller life. Gratitude has optimal benefits for everybody.

If you're new to acknowledging your gratitude daily, let me share the method I share with others. Consider getting yourself a three-ring binder or spiral notebook. I know that for many of you, a pen and paper are archaic. However, you'll feel more connected when you write with a pen to paper. You could even get one of those small notebooks to write in for those who travel. Here are the steps:

1. Get the notebook or, if need be, a laptop or iPad.

2. For the first thirty days, write down a minimum of three things you are grateful for each day. Take a moment to reflect on how they make you feel grateful.

3. Each day before you begin your day, quickly review a few thoughts you have previously written.

4. Then check a few more each evening before you write down three more that night.

5. Repeat for thirty days.

6. Then continue or repeat periodically.

Also, don't be concerned if you can't think of any new ones; they'll appear in time. Repeat some of your other statements with the meaning changed. You know how your English teacher used to emphasize that if you wrote a sentence one way, it meant this, but if you moved the comma over here, it had a different interpretation?

I can hear some of you resisting already. "But Cathy, what if I forget or can't do that every day?"

I'd probably candidly answer, "You do what you're capable of. You're accountable for your actions. I believe you'll get out of this program what you put into this program. I suggest you do the best you can."

I also believe a few slip-ups won't hurt, provided you quickly get back on schedule. The problem lies in getting back on track. Many people seem to be resistant about doing so. I suggest doing your best to stay focused for thirty days. If you miss one, it's best to get back on track quickly. After the first thirty days, most of you will see the rewards. You'll notice many positive changes, such as an improved attitude, clarity, confidence, feeling happier, and being more self-assured.

Now you can decide how you want to continue implementing this technique in your life. Even though this seems simplistic, implementing daily action can produce miraculous changes. Some people continue this routine. Another suggestion is to pull out your notebook a few times a week and add any new ones or even reminders. Plus, read over it several times weekly, reminding you what to be thankful for. Lastly, work and update your journal anytime from time to time, especially when you need some recentering or empowerment.

Some have asked, "What if I'm not grateful or I don't see any changes within thirty days?"

Perhaps you're not mindfully expressing gratitude. I don't believe I've ever had someone not experience some appreciation. However, I'm sure some folks will not. Reread what you wrote down in the last thirty days. Are you expressing gratitude? You may need to think deeper, focus more, and imagine the possibilities.

After doing a mindfulness exercise with Erika, she retrieved her journal. As suggested, she wrote down five things she was grateful for, which seemed difficult initially. She read them aloud to me. She expanded on what they meant to her, and she seemed to feel serenity as she did so. The tension in her facial muscles relaxed as she stated she was feeling much better. I suggested she review some of her journal entries then pick some to discuss.

As she continued sharing her thoughts, she joyously expressed gratitude when one entry reminded her she was more resilient than she was giving herself credit for. She also shared she was easing her thoughts as she reread and discussed entries that brought her more clarity and awareness. That day, as Erika reviewed what she was grateful for, I witnessed a positive and beautiful life-changing transformation. She left the session with a sense of profound serenity and confidence. Erika showed me how she could utilize the Attitude of Gratitude journal writing as a positive resource to help her experience faith and trust in the world daily. She showed herself this tool would help her develop and build a resilient self. A resilient self can assist her with bouncing back quickly from victimhood, along with confronting the many other future trials and tribulations that will make their way into her life.

If you haven't done so already, grab a notebook and label it "An Attitude of Gratitude Journal" or whatever sounds like being grateful to you. Then twice a day, usually in the morning and evening, write down at least three things you are thankful exist. If you initially have trouble with this, please use any of the suggested ideas. As you work on this over time, your thankfulness will expand. Then each morning, upon rising, read over a few entries from your notebook. As stated previously, as you do this activity more often, you will begin noticing more things you are grateful for throughout the day. For instance, you might be enlightened when walking by a beautiful garden and realizing how grateful you are for the scenery and the ability to smell the fresh flowers' lush scent. You may wonder why you hadn't noticed this before, even though you have often passed by this garden.

When you desire to live a more prosperous life, whatever that may be for you, your transformation will be more challenging if you're not an open-minded and optimistic person. Applying this method helps you become more receptive to the possibilities. Implementing positive concepts in your toolbox to assist you in building your mindset flexibility is the goal of these methods. As Bob Doyle states, quoting from *The Secret* by Rhonda Byrne, "…. the law of attraction says that like attracts like. But we're talking at a level of thought." Improving upon these strategies is vital for creating your resilient foundation and stronger emotional resilience, clarity, and positive energy. Therefore, you become more of the person you wish to attract into your life.

Many people desiring a more prosperous lifestyle are, like Erika was, still in the struggle. They have excellent intentions. They want changes, yet they need to learn how to obtain them. Transforming is much like a musician learning to play the piano. At first, a person, usually a young child, learns the mechanics;

then one learns easy songs, and of course, they practice hours each month, year after year. In the beginning, there was the struggle of learning new material and disciplining oneself to practice. They accomplished more challenging material with guidance and perseverance. Over time, they learned to play many entertaining songs well. By diligently practicing, they have acquired mastery. Daily playing has been integrated into their lifestyle because they enjoy doing so. Thus, their mindset has changed and shifted over time. And yours can, too, with the proper guidance and much practice every day.

You now have An Attitude of Gratitude Journal to add to your toolbox.

Chapter 5

Affirmations & Slogans

For me, the patterns and disturbing thoughts holding me back revolved around everything in my life. At the time, despite having just received my master's degree, my biggest hindrances were low self-esteem and low self-worth. Both of these showed up many times as "fear" and "shame" in my life back then. Whether or not it was warranted, that is how I felt and reacted to those difficulties. I was having trouble getting out of my way.

Have you ever noticed a recurring pattern of thoughts or feelings, like a theme? If you have seen similar reoccurrences, reflect upon your behavior and beliefs. Are you engaging in activities that you hold to you to your values, or are you engaging in activities that devalue you? Consistent thinking and behavior are standard, but if they are consistently extremely harmful or destructive behavior or thinking, consider seeking a professional. Unfortunately, books cannot evaluate people, so please talk to someone if you are experiencing distressing reoccurrences. However, I do want to emphasize I didn't grasp the connection between my thoughts, feelings, and reactions for a long while. It is challenging to step out of yourself and objectively observe and note your behavior, right? All I knew was that I wanted to live differently. I began seeking and applying short-term solutions that seemed to appear as I was traversing along my journey. These undertakings seemed to assist with processing my healing and mending my soul.

I am sharing this with you because perhaps you can relate, as I connected to Louise's stories and information as if she were speaking to me. Looking back, I realize some of her stories validated my circumstances. Through her stories, I became hopeful as I understood myself better. Even though I had read previous self-help books, Louise Hay's stories resonated with and moved me.

They inspired me to take action. For the first time that I remember, I saw possibilities for me. I realized I, too, could escape trapped situations. I could improve my life, and I did not need to feel guilty for doing so. So, my life began transforming little by little. I became more open, forgiving, and accepting of situations, past and present. Even though I had read other influencers' work previously, I needed help finding their solutions for me. Their material was interesting, but I believed their suggestions only worked for those "other" people, not me. Somehow though, I never truly gave up. When I found Louise's books, her words spoke to me in a way that made sense. I was ready to learn, and she intuitively knew what to share with me. She had simplistic ideas that worked. I was thrilled. Interestingly enough, her writings appeared as I was finishing the first promise I had made to myself; I was about to earn my master's degree.

Louise's methods consisted of positive affirmations. When I learned about those affirmations and began implementing them, I could see and feel my life positively moving. I noticed increased self-assuredness and confidence. My perspective was shifting, and I realized I understood myself better than I had previously. I felt relieved, and rejuvenated and ready for new adventures. Living and thinking more positively was exciting and created new opportunities for me. Doing so brought newfound hope.

Affirmations are positive statements that you create for yourself. These comprise of your hopes, dreams, and wishes. You write them down in the present tense as if they have already happened. Then you state them out loud, usually looking yourself in the eyes using a mirror several times a day. Even though you understand they are not confirmed yet, you say them out loud and with conviction as if they already are. With consistency and repetition, you are changing your personal beliefs and increasing your energy level as you regularly practice.

I remember writing down word for word, the words right out of her book. I would then get in front of my mirror and carefully listen as I read the paper out loud. I felt nervous and felt like an imposter. At first, I couldn't even look at myself in the mirror. I remember doubting that reciting these statements aloud, over and over again, would make a difference. I knew these statements weren't accurate. I thought, "What if they didn't become true?" However, a small inkling inside me urged me to keep going, so I did.

As I stated the affirmations, I saw slow progress. Even though a significant development was transforming, I would easily get distracted by daily busyness. Still, as I persevered, I began raising my head and looking at myself in the mirror. My courage began to flicker, and I became more empowered. I saw myself becoming more hopeful, confident, and self-assured. My life was positively transforming, and I was amazed. At last, I knew I was moving positively forward with my circumstances.

Mottos and clichés are handy little blurbs you can use interchangeably to help others or yourself make sense of or cope with a situation. I know some people get irritated at hearing some of these phrases. However, I have found they are a quick remedy, easy to apply, and you can quickly memorize them for easy access. While working with clients, I have been known to detect specific affirmations or clichés unique to their needs.

They serve a healthy purpose when utilized correctly. Their meanings' can motivate or inspire you to reach goals, be determined, ease heartaches, foster hope, and keep living forward, depending on your situation. For example, "when God closes one door, He opens another" is a great slogan you can use when some circumstances change in your life. Case in point, God nudged me at a bookstore I was visiting just as I closed the door on my educational career.

While looking around for a book to purchase, unsure of what I wanted, I walked by this bookshelf, and I felt this sudden urge to pull a particular book off the shelf as if the book had literally jumped out at me. I quickly glanced through the book. I didn't recall seeing it before. It seemed inspiring, so I bought it. And as I began reading Louise Hay's book, I realized her information would guide me through another step in my journey. Her stories made sense and resonated with me. I related to her dilemmas. I thought, "If this worked for her and others, why would it not work for me?" As I am telling my story, I hope you are hearing things that resonate with you.

"Everything in life happens for a reason" is another adage many people spout. This motto can be applied when people experience happy or sad times. For example, working with many people, I have repeatedly seen and heard personal stories of how people will continue similar negative actions until something circumvents the process. Thus, some patterns continue until the person learns and confronts that challenge. This adage can be applied to detach yourself from specific circumstances. Other mottos I find helpful for many people are "this too shall pass," which is excellent for moving through difficult times. Another favorite is "let go, let God." And I am sure there are many more. You may research and find others you like better than what has been mentioned here.

Slogans – Your Dictionary (Online) states, "The definition of a slogan is "a distinctive cry, phrase, or motto of any party, group, manufacturer, or person; catchword or catch phrase." You can utilize these when you need to improve your mentality and energy. You will memorize what will remind or motivate you to do so. Create something easy to recall, such as using catchy mottos and slogans that elevate your mood, are quick to memorize and recite, keeps you focused, or transforms you through difficult situations.

Thus, this book provides information to assist you with living a better life. Successful people integrate these components so that they may live their best lives. You can too.

So think about your relationships, work career, and lifestyle. Are you content and happy in those areas of your life? Do you desire more wealth, prosperity, and abundance? Your ability to change your mindset and put yourself into a position to increase your finances are possible. What do you want your life to look and be like five years from now? For instance, do you want to improve your relationships? Maybe you have healthy and satisfying relationships but feel like something is amiss. You may want to discover your next career step. Are you looking for a better work-life balance with great co-workers? Do you need to feel more empowered, self-confident, and courageous? Do you want to conquer some of your limiting beliefs, such as fear and self-criticism, to be more assertive? Would you like to quit second-guessing yourself?

Most importantly, you may not know the particulars about what you need. You can still figure out what to do. You just keep moving forward and learning and changing as you go along. As I stated earlier, I did not know either. I just knew something had to change, and I was going to make that change happen. Embarking on your self-discovery journey involves experiencing an open mind and creating increased self-awareness. Next, implement some of these or other similar slogans into your life. Choose a few that resonate with you and begin stating them aloud daily. As you implement that action, with patience and insight, you will understand which ones work best for you. Your situation and perception will help you connect with the ones you need to apply now, and later, you will discover which others work for you. Using these slogans helps you manage your mind or help you grow, learn and change. Use them accordingly. With time and belief, applying these slogans will help you uncover and heal more pieces than you may understand now.

So you may be thinking about what affirmations are and why they work. Positive affirmations are present tense statements affirming something you wish to become or improve. Stating them out loud can change your actions, perception, and moods. Some changes may be quick, while others take time to process. Reasonable and small achievable affirmations are easy to apply and can produce excellent results.

Most people will notice changes right away. Here are a few examples: "I am happy. I am worthy! I love my life." Any changes depend on your effort, readiness for change, transition and perception. For instance, if you state I have an attentive loving husband and you are not married, other things directly involved will need to happen before this will, such as meeting the right man. You may ask. You may believe it. Changes may need to occur to prepare you. Timing and circumstances are involved too. Thus, everything happens for a reason.

So, how do you create these, or where can you find some affirmations? You may visit my website and sign up for my email list. I send several out to my email list each month. However, making up your own to apply to your situations is helpful. Affirmations are positive present tense statements as if they are already confirmed. Here is how to create positive affirmations for yourself or others.

Creating Self-Affirming Statements:

- You speculate and conclude the positive asset or goal you want to obtain.

- You create a present tense sentence aiming for those results.

For instance, Deanna states she is shy and wishes to be more vibrant and courageous. Her sentences would sound something like this: "I am outgoing. I am courageous. I adore meeting new people. I am vivacious. I have an open-minded perception."

-   Next, Deanna needs to write her statements down.

-   Then she looks at herself in the mirror and states these statements aloud daily.

-   Most importantly, Deanna makes eye contact with herself as she says each of these.

-   She repeats these affirmations three times in the morning and three times in the evening.

Then Deanna begins confidently looking herself in her eyes as she gains more certainty. These steps are excellent for you too.

For example, if you think you feel unworthy or not good enough, some suggestions might be: "I am worthy, important, and good enough just as I am." If you are working towards a job promotion, the statements might be, "I am intelligent; I am excellent at my job, and I can learn new things quickly. Along with these statements, my performance is high; My bosses believe my work ethic and performance are excellent, and I am the new _____. "(Fill in the blank). Of course, if you have more details, feel free to embellish these statements. It is best to have present tense, focused, and clear messages for the paramount results. Begin with the result you wish to achieve and write a simple sentence using "I" statements in the present tense as if you have already achieved the desired results.

Some may think this message is false, so you think you can't say that. You are correct. But you want the statement to become true for you. To move you forward in that direction, you need to state the sentence as if it is true daily. Also, some people may need to process more work or actions before they are ready to receive the solution. For instance, Deanna experienced more situations in her life, which helped her prepare for her results. You may need more time or be given more challenges to prepare you to be ready for the results.

To recap - Positive affirmations are present tense statements affirming something you wish to become or improve. Stating them out loud can change your actions, perception, and moods. Some changes may be quick, while others take time to process. Reasonable and small achievable affirmations are easy to apply. Significant changes depend on your effort, readiness for change, transition, and perception. However, with minor applications, you may notice shifts right away.

Why do I suggest mottos and slogans? As you move throughout your day, your moods change quickly. It is best to have some simple strategies for negative energy moods to regain your positive energy. Slogans and mottos are other strategies to assist you with staying in a better frame of mind. Life happens. You might need refreshers or boosters, which can be slogans or mottos. Creating some trivial 'upbeat' slogans and stating them in your head or aloud a few times can quickly change a person's mood. Hopefully, the results will be for the better.

For example, suppose Deanna shares she quickly gets frustrated at work, and her mood usually flattens out in the afternoon. Here are other slogans for her. "Let Go, Let God; this too shall pass; one step at a time; and I can put one foot in front of the other; all is well in my world." She can add some affirmations, such as "Every day in every way, my work environment is better and better; and every day in every way, I am efficient and friendly. Some of these may be similar to her other mottos or affirmations. That is fine.

Mottos and slogans can also be applied when events or situations are upsetting or confusing. If you react negatively to these situations, your reactions may negatively impact your mood. It could lead you not to be your best and get off track. Often this issue can be negated when you apply slogans or affirmations, such as: "All is well in my world." or "I calmly and assertively challenge that mistake."

Have you ever experienced some similar mood changes, such as these?

You got passed over for a promotion.

Your car breaks down when you rely on your vehicle daily.

Your child is experiencing negative issues at school.

You are frustrated with your child's school policies.

One of your parents just went to the emergency room.

A co-worker disappointed you.

Your spouse had a bad day and brought that negativism home.

Something will always arise, but you can lessen the negative mental agony of your circumstances by staying in a positive mindset, such as "this too shall pass." With consistency and repetition, you can strengthen your mental stamina. You will become less emotionally attached to situations when doing so. Sometimes you may even use the slogan – "that is life or oh, the joys of life." These aid you in recognizing and accepting the situation without judgment.

Utilizing positive affirmations and helpful slogans when you need to recuperate your mentality and energy is an excellent skill. You memorize what will remind or motivate you to ease a situation you experience. Create something easy to recall, such as using catchy mottos and slogans that elevate your mood, keep you focused, or transform you through difficult situations.

Implementing these can be a game-changer for you. If you are a swearing type, slogans can keep you from constantly swearing and producing negative vibes. You can create funny sayings, too, so everybody laughs, increasing the positive vibes. Plus, slogans are easy to recall and can be used now. Remember, these techniques will only work if applied. Take a moment and write down a few you will use. You can use the ones presented in this chapter. There are also two written on the first page of Chapter One. You can look some up on the Internet or come up with your own. Make them fun and easy to remember.

Your results depend on your actions, meaning you get what you put into something. Now that's a cliché. However, do not fret if you forget or get too busy. You can be flexible, but write down a date to begin soon if you are not ready. Keep your commitment for that date. You may need to change your affirmations and mottos from time to time as situations change or they get boring. Remember to be flexible with yourself and your circumstances. Think about these two mottos – "Take one step at a time and never give up." Hopefully, these mottos will be easier to apply than you thought.

You will have different experiences, perceptions, needs, and responses. However, you are encouraged to try these methods even if you don't foresee needing them. Many of you will be amazed at the changes you acquire in a brief amount of time. One of the most incredible experiences is getting noticeable results you didn't even realize you needed. Positive affirmations and slogans work. Most people, including you, can navigate through life's challenges more successfully with these than without them. If you are not already using them, please begin these simple actions today! Don't wait any longer; seize the moment.

Chapter 6

Positive Thinking
Reframing Your Negative Thinking

Our perception is influenced and conditioned by our environment, especially during our early childhood years. Most of our reasoning and thought-provoking actions originate from our perceptions, whether or not they are conscious to us. Some thoughts will be positive, and others will be negative. According to cognitive behavioral therapy, our actions or lack of actions are created by our thoughts.

In this chapter, we're concerned about the destructive thoughts affecting your belief system and your best living. Several theories support the idea that our beliefs determine what we can be and do. "What the mind of man can conceive and believe, it can achieve." Says Napoleon Hill. (Hill, 2007) With that quote in mind, we could conclude that people live their lives based on their beliefs.

What if you don't know your life could be better? What if you realize you know but are stuck in the resistance you keep telling yourself? We all experience optimistic thoughts, at least now and then. Don't you wonder why you can't be upbeat all the time?

Would you like to experience your best thinking so that you're living your best life?

You may wonder why you're challenged to move beyond cynical and negative thinking, and if only you could squash those pesky thoughts. This chapter aims to present common negative thoughts, share how that thinking can negatively impact your life, and provide strategies for overcoming that type of thinking so that you can live more successfully.

Shortly after I began working in the counseling arena, it became apparent that people accepted their limitations as facts. Of course, there are exceptions, but many people believe their limitations define them, and their lives evolve around those limitations. Experiencing limiting beliefs close many opportunities for them because their perception accepts that nothing can or will change. People can create and attain a perception of themselves, whether the results are negative or positive. Then, they might argue that this is how they've been all their lives. Listening to their stories and reasons validates how powerful the mind's thoughts can be. Beautiful, smart, intelligent people believe that their thoughts became their truth because they thought something. They focused on their shortcomings, which became their forever truth. They didn't know about other possibilities because they focused on assuming the worst, arguing for their restrictions, feeling like victims, and accepting their circumstances as something that doesn't change. They live their lives around these thoughts.

If you can identify with this, you're not alone. Setting limitations or defending your current circumstances is common, especially in the US. However, there is hope. If you were to change your thinking, can you imagine new possibilities that might arise?

There are many cons when you experience limited belief thinking. As I stated earlier, many people are resistant and argue for their ability to remain the same. They believe there's no other strategy, or they "can't do it." Living with that reasoning in mind might be comfortable and familiar for that person; thus, they overlook other options.

When I met Maureen, a beautiful yet crushed woman, she argued for her limitations due to her misfortunes. She believed she was worthless and claimed she wouldn't amount to anything. I noticed an intelligent young woman who had lost her way and trust in others. However, here she was, trusting me with her story. As she continued speaking, I heard a brilliant, caring, articulate young mother pouring her heart out to me. As she worked through her paperwork in my office, I wondered why she thought she couldn't overcome her unfortunate circumstances. Questions began popping up in my head. Why was she recommended for outpatient treatment? I wonder if her thoughts were holding her back and pretending to keep her safe. Does she feel unworthy now because she knew better? Does her mind feed her lies because she made a mistake? What is stopping Maureen from moving positively forward? What story is she possibly rehearsing over and over in her mind?

Consider how your beliefs might hinder you when walking through a specific challenging situation. People gravitate toward familiarity regardless of whether it's a safe and happy place or not. Thus, people will continue living with what is familiar and comfortable. Some people become cynical, carrying out their best living in a state they have mentally outgrown. Other people find themselves in a "push and pull" scenario where they're most likely living with resistance. They're trying to push away from the situation but are being pulled back due to many things. If you're reading this book, you've probably navigated through many challenges. Changes are common and usually happen without noticing, such as children transitioning to higher classes each year. However, other times changes can be challenging and emotionally painful. Regardless of the path, the fact is change is inevitable.

Utilizing the information above, think about what you do when you face challenges. Do you quickly move forward? Are you

49

resistant for whatever reason? Who are you when you can no longer bear the pain? Practical people will face the challenge and make the necessary changes. Other people will rise and meet their resistance in certain conditions when they're ready to move on. Some people leave the situation, and some will never make any changes.

As you can infer, Maureen's story began years before she came to the outpatient clinic where I worked. Her mindset was not strong enough to overcome the defeating thoughts that caused her to think less of herself. The more deflated she felt, the easier it was for her to justify living in a situation she didn't align with, such as getting involved with the wrong people. Her thoughts and actions were moving her in the wrong direction. However, when Maureen focuses on changing her mindset, she realizes she can overcome challenges and set healthier boundaries. Whether or not you're in a highly challenging situation, you can utilize what Maureen learned to better yourself. These tools are universal and can be used by anyone at any stage in their life. Maureen's story illustrates a stark contrast between her current ways of living and thinking versus how she improves her life by addressing her thinking and changing her actions. For some of you, your life is going well, but you want to enhance bits of it. These concepts can help you improve your outlook and life.

For instance, one of my first jobs as a mental health counselor began in the alcohol and drug treatment unit at our local state psychiatric facility. I facilitated intakes and group treatment for many alcohol and drug-addicted folks for several years. The stats for addiction recovery rates are not very hopeful; one in four will be successful. Watching many intelligent and wonderful people relapse and not return to finish the treatment protocol is heartbreaking for them and me. Other people, such as family members, are more confused and wonder why they return to such activities. Their relatives often question, "What's calling them back to a life many don't want to live? Why can't they leave?" And the one in four that successfully finished might be the one everyone least expected. You might be curious as to what separates those who recover and those who don't.

Several justifications can be determined. Here are a few:

Memories entangled with past emotions.

Ideas such as not being able to live without something.

Fear.

Believing using was the only place they felt accepted.

Another reason is that something familiar can be easy to return to, such as being around people drinking and using in earlier years.

Their minds and bodies may be physically addicted.

And several other reasons for another book.

The point to recognize is every person has something in common. Each person is experiencing resistance despite their best intentions. Some will overcome their opposition, and many will not.

Let's look at the case with Maureen. Maureen was referred to our treatment program because her lifestyle was failing her. She was on the verge of losing custody of her children to the state. Maureen was in trouble with the law, too. She needed to change her life while overcoming her substance abuse.

During the intake assessment, I learned a lot about Maureen. As I listened intently, I heard a tiny ray of desire left inside her as she talked. She shared that she desperately wanted to get clean, stay clean, and get away from those other people. She confessed she hated living this way and wanted things to be better for her and her children. The more she shared, the more she needed to share. She poured her story out to me as I quietly listened, nodding here and there.

Then she broke down, releasing massive tears and loud cries that seemed to be arising from her soul. She was letting out that agony and pain she'd been holding all these years. She could no longer hold back. That moment was her turning point. She was ready for her transformation. She was a strong survivor, knowing she had experienced so much deep down inside. However, despite those actions, she shared that she didn't see her life changing even though she was taking steps to improve it. She said what she said but knew she was at a turning point. She couldn't admit it, yet.

I reassured her there was hope. I suggested she give this program a chance. "If not for you, for your children."

After some reflection, she refocused herself and stated she would. I assured her everything was all right and would be all right. "It's time to take care of you and your family. No apology is needed."

She looked up at me and nodded. There might have even been a glimpse of hope in her eyes.

What if you didn't need to wait until you felt like you were against a brick wall to make those changes? What if you didn't have to experience too much pain or mental anguish to create positive changes or walk through resistance? What if your resistance led to and allowed changes to be an easier-flowing transition? What if your joy begins inside you and not with outsiders? Your life doesn't have to be in shambles before you act.

As I mentioned in the last chapter, what you think matters. What if I told you, "You are what you think you are"? Then you have two choices. Either accept who you are being or change your thinking. Stating positive self-talk daily can improve your mental belief system and affect how you perceive and live your life. As stated in Matthew 7:7-8 "Ask, and it will be given to you; seek, and you will find, knock and it will be opened to you. For everyone who acts receives, and he who seeks find, and to him who knocks it will be opened." This scripture is true for everybody. What are you asking for and seeking? Are you ready to improve your way of thinking?

Remember, people have tried to convince me they are what they think they are. People quickly get stuck in their narrow thinking. No one is immune to this phenomenon. However, research and case studies have demonstrated people can overcome their belief limitations. Even the law of attraction is about what you think you create and attract into your life. Also, as specified by Norman Vincent Peale, 'In the first place, you must believe it can be done" from *Positive Imaging: The Powerful Way to Change Your Life* (1982, p. 67). Thus, to maintain a healthy lifestyle or reach a new plateau, adding positive affirmations can be the catalyst for rewarding transitions. What would those possibilities mean for you?

Now that you understand positive thinking is powerful, please think about this. What are the words and meanings of the information you tell yourself daily? Do your thoughts keep you trapped in a negative thinking pattern, or are you empowered by your messages? Be honest with yourself. When rummaging through your daily thoughts, what do you recognize? Do you hear something stopping you from acting?

Do you ever argue with someone, and you know you're right? How can you be sure? Could both of you be right? Take some time and examine your thoughts. Then reflect upon your self-talk. Your perception of life is just that, your life perception.

Positive self-talk is very effective in healing your mind, body, and spirit. For instance, some cancer survivors stated they utilized visualizations along with positive healing affirmations to put their cancer in remission. Accepting the belief that positive thoughts are essential to living your best life, what ideas would you like to change? You might recognize some easily. Pay closer attention to what your thinking tells you every day and when experiencing different situations. As stated previously, think about the actual words and meanings of the information you tell

53

yourself daily. Do those thoughts keep you trapped in negative thinking, such as feeling defeated or overwhelmed, or are you empowered by your messages, such as feeling confident and focused? At first, some may be challenging to analyze, but as you begin with little steps, others will become more apparent.

All communication is essential, including communicating with others. What do you say or think about others? Are any of the thoughts condescending beliefs? If so, it will be vital to include those statements in the Recognizing and Reframing exercise. Honestly, I don't believe a person cannot stop thinking negatively at times, but the point of this book is to help you feel positive and live a better life. This chapter teaches you about obvious negative thoughts that negatively affect you or the people you surround yourself with. Communication with yourself, your self-talk, communication with others, and what you think or say are important.

You must be mindful of your self-talk and your communications with others to begin recovering from self-sabotaging thoughts or other negative thinking. This includes all negative thoughts like "I don't think I can," "He's a jerk," and "I'm too shy," along with millions of others. Please note what you say to yourself or others in response to what you thought or what they said.

Get yourself a 3-ring binder or spiral notebook and begin writing down any negative thoughts for a minimum of seven days. Throughout your day and with your conversations with others, listen for those negative thoughts or responses that are diverting or negatively impacting you, such as "I can't do that or that will never work." When you hear such a phrase or feel that resistance, please take a moment to write down your thoughts or what you just negatively stated. You don't need to concern yourself with why you thought or said that now. The first step is learning to recognize negative thinking and positively reframe it into empowered thoughts.

Doing this exercise for at least seven days will tremendously assist you in realizing your negative thoughts/patterns. Over time you'll probably identify more negative thought patterns, or you may decide to work with a life coach to help you. Don't be hard on yourself. Allow yourself some grace. It's imperative to note you're not attempting to go through your mind and wipe it clean of every negative thought you think. It would be best if you had patience with this exercise and consistency for the best results.

Now begin a new section in your notebook at the end of seven days. Divide this sheet into two columns and write at the top of your paper. Name one column: **"The Negative Statements"** and the second column **"My New Positive Statements."** (See diagram.) You may think of this exercise as recognizing and reframing these thoughts. You can also do this assignment on a digital device. Many people have better results with handwriting this assignment rather than using digital devices. Thus, I suggest handwriting this for the best results.

Write down in your first column all your negative statements. Go to the bar right below so you can stay on the left of the page if there isn't enough room on the line. Work on writing down your negative statements until you've covered everything you noticed.

Now, look at your sentence, and in your My New Positive Statements column next to it, write down how you could rephrase your statement by using the opposite meaning. These will be positive statements in the present tense as if they are true. Here are a few simplistic examples:

"The Negative Statements" "My New Positive Statements"

Recognize Reframe

"I can't" will be changed to "I can."

"I am afraid." to "I am courageous."

"I don't know how." to "I can learn."

55

Please note: Your new positive statements will not feel true to you. That is normal because, initially, they're not. The intention is to help them become true as you state them aloud.

The next step is to take three or four of your new affirmations and state these aloud three times daily as you look at yourself in the mirror. As you notice your self-talk positively changing, add others to your system.

Once you hear yourself speaking or thinking positively without thinking about it, you'll know you're on the right track. As you progress, you can add or subtract these ideas as needed. Now, you're on the path to changing your thinking in a more positive direction.

As you improve your thoughts and communication, you can experience healthier relationships and lifestyles. You'll notice a difference with just one or two changes. For those who recognize you need to create more positive thoughts, doing so will help you create sustaining, life-altering healthy habits to help you perform your best. The neatest thing is people in your life will notice. As Napoleon Hill claimed in the 1961 edition of his book, *Think and Grow Rich,* "Our thinking is powerful and gives us ideas of what we can obtain by changing our thoughts." Now it's time to get your pen and paper and begin.

Maureen began her new journey working on her mindset. She worked with her perspective first. She dove in, and immediately positive results appeared due to her efforts. Maureen created a notebook like the one described earlier and worked on it daily. Then she added a thankful and positive affirmations section to the notebook.

As she began practicing, people noticed she seemed more optimistic. Her confidence began to shine, and she seemed determined to regain herself. She set weekly goals and worked hard at obtaining them. She believed she could, so she did. Maureen was a role model for anyone she encountered. She did well, and she changed her life for the better.

Chapter 7

Mindfulness and Meditation

Mindfulness is observing your thoughts and emotions so that you're aware of what you're thinking, feeling, and experiencing. Dr. Richard Nongard, author and hypnosis expert, states that mindfulness means paying attention to the present and giving attention to the present in a nonjudgmental way (Nongard, 2010). He further claims that living mindfully helps you live fully in the present—today and not tomorrow. Being mindful "is a quality that's associated with many mental health benefits and other positive attributes, such as self-esteem and self-acceptance" (Thompson & Waltz, 2007, as cited in Schultz 2023). Overall, mindfulness has many positive qualities, such as helping you focus, reduce stress, improve sleep, reduce panic attacks, and live a more fulfilling life.

Mindfulness is the simple process of focusing your mind. Meditation is an intentional practice where you focus on a particular outcome, such as calmness, concentration, and emotional balance. Meditation doesn't mean you're practicing mindfulness, but mindfulness meditation is a strategy for practicing both.

Mindfulness and meditation are excellent concepts for clearing mental clutter and re-centering yourself. Both are helpful with decreasing stressful symptoms and emotional mood swings, increasing your focus and clarity, increasing satisfaction and serenity, and increasing your well-being and health. Thus, research demonstrates that both methods have shown many positive mind, body, and spiritual benefits.

Meditations and mindfulness meditations are easy to apply and provide quick positive solutions for some issues. As a solution-focused coach, I had difficulty learning how to meditate. I'd find myself more tense and frustrated because I couldn't experience meditation in what I presumed to be the "right way." Years later, I learned to practice short methods for three to five minutes daily with the ability to add more time if I chose. This chapter focuses on these applications. You may find these specific techniques helpful, too.

"I'm concerned. My boss has been understanding and patient with my issue, but I'm not sure how much longer he will be. I don't like having this condition! I didn't used to experience these panic attacks. Why now? I don't know how long my boss will be patient; I have difficulty being patient," Mark exclaimed.

Mark shared he's a happily married man and the father of two children. He likes his job and can't see himself doing anything else. Mark reported all had been going well until he unknowingly began having panic attacks almost a year ago. He said he thought he was experiencing a heart attack when they started. He has been to the emergency room and also saw his physician for the same complaints. "No one is finding anything medically wrong," he reported.

After thorough medical testing and evaluation, his physician informed him that he believes he's suffering from panic attacks consisting of symptoms of extreme anxiety attacks and elevated heart rates. His doctor prescribed anxiety medication which was supposed to fix the attacks.

Mark continued, "Now, three months later, nothing has changed." He said he tried the medication, but the attacks have not decreased. Plus, he reported he didn't like taking the medication. "Taking this prescription makes me feel drowsy, and I'm not operating at my best." He claimed he felt scattered and couldn't think clearly. "I need to be able to focus for my presentations," he reported. Since he was still experiencing his panic attacks, or so they are called, he claimed, "I don't want this medication."

He shared, "I don't know what caused them, and I don't know what to do about them either. My job requires me to travel a lot. I had to cancel flights twice because of these attacks. These are interrupting my work, and they seem to be getting worse! I'm concerned. As I said earlier, I don't know how long my employer will be patient with me. I may need to look for another line of work. I'm limited as to what I can do. I was informed you could help me. You're my last resort." I acknowledged as we continued his assessment.

Whether you're experiencing panic attacks, too much stress and tension, low self-esteem, poor parenting, and numerous other issues, learning and practicing short meditations have shown to be helpful for many people. Research has shown that practicing meditation is beneficial for multiple medical diagnoses, such as diabetes, cancer treatments, general illness, and surgeries, to name a few. Practicing meditation has also increased self-confidence, self-worth, clarity, and concentration and can help decrease stress. Many people claim they receive great results with the aid of meditating. Research has shown that practicing long-term meditation has many health and well-being benefits.

So what about you? Is your quality of life affected by stress, tension, difficulty concentrating, or the other numerous things I mentioned? Have you noticed that your quality of life suffers?

What if you could live a better quality of life? Practicing meditation may be the solution you need. Adding this solution to your toolbox is relatively easy. You only need three to five minutes a day and be willing to be open to changes. Here are the steps:

BREATHWORK

Correct breathing is essential for mindfulness meditation and other meditation work. The first thing is to begin with correct breathing.

Take a moment and think about how you breathe. Do your shoulders and chest expand when you do so? If so, this needs to be improved. You're not releasing all your tension as you do so. A better way is to learn belly breathing, where your abdomen will rise up and fall down as you breathe in and out. Belly breathing increases your oxygen intake, relaxes your body, and helps keep you healthy. Think about babies sleeping soundly. Have you ever noticed their little bellies rise up and down as they breathe in and out? They are breathing correctly. You were born breathing correctly too. However, many of us changed our breathing techniques as we grew older, especially as we experienced stressful situations.

Pick a quiet place in your home or office where you are free from distractions.

1. Sit in a supportive chair where you're comfortable sitting up straight as you plant your feet firmly on the ground. Being free of distractions is essential. You may also be lying down or sitting on the floor cross-legged, but being in a supportive chair is best for many people.

2. Sit up straight. Refrain from hunching if you can.

3. Now, focus on your breathwork. Clasp your hands and lay them gently across your belly button. When correctly breathing, your hands will move up with every inhale and down with every exhale. Now take a slow deep breath in, and as you do, you can feel the rise in your abdomen as

if you're filling a balloon. If it's not rising, exaggerate the belly expansion on the next breath and feel it rise with your hands. Do this until you're aware your deep breaths are filling your lungs, and you notice the rise of your abdomen as you breathe in and the fall as you breathe out. Practice this method until you're breathing properly.

4. Once you have mastered the breathwork technique, you can begin the meditation.

5. Now, as you sit in the chair or lie on the floor, you may keep your eyes open or closed. Think of your breathing and how it feels in your body. You'll take a slow deep gentle breath through the nostrils and slowly release it through the mouth. The only thing you need to concentrate on is your breathing. As you're slowly breathing in and out a few times, notice how your body is feeling.

6. Now, scan your body and release any tension as you breathe in and out. Many people begin at the top of their head, move to the face, neck, shoulders, and arms, and work toward their feet. Then they release the built-up tension or negative energy out through the feet and then the toes. Others work up from their toes to the crown of their head. Choose what feels best for you.

7. Concentrate on your air intake, expanding your abdomen like a balloon and shrinking your balloon as you exhale. Do this for one to three minutes. Great! You have now mastered your first meditation.

Congratulations! Do you notice any tension relief? What about more clarity and focus? You may have felt a more profound sense of gratification. Over time, with your consistent practice, you'll notice positive changes. Now that you have completed the proper breathwork, you're ready to try other short meditations.

Mark claimed that teaching him basic meditation techniques improved his life. We worked on deep breathing meditation, relaxation, and visualization techniques that first day in my office. He was instructed to take this home and practice every day. When he came to see me a week later, his face appeared more relaxed, as if all his tension had disappeared from it. He shared that he was much more relieved and relaxed. He assured me he could overcome these panic attacks easily now.

Mark began applying these meditations whenever he needed to relax or recenter himself. He claimed doing so was relatively easy and less challenging than he imagined when he was initially introduced to them. Over time, he regained his composure and seemed much happier.

For the following techniques, use the breathwork technique and setup. Find a quiet place without distractions and a comfortable, supportive chair. Plant your feet firmly on the ground. Sit upright as best as you can and apply the proper breathing procedure. On the in-breath, slowly breathe in through your nose, and as you exhale, breathe out through your mouth. If you have difficulty, do the best you can and move on.

Relaxation Meditation: When ready, make a strong fist with one of your hands. Hold the fist so tight for a brief moment that you begin to feel pain slightly. Now gently release. Your body feels that tightness from the tension you felt. When you release the fist, did you notice your hand relaxed? Now do this again and be mindful of the pressure you're creating. Then notice the relaxed feeling upon releasing. How was that experience? Great! Now take a moment and scan your body for other tension. When you find some, apply this same technique of gently tightening the pressure, then releasing the tension two to three times. Create enough tension for you to notice and then relax. Do this in moderation. Each time you do so, do you feel the area you're concentrating on becoming more relaxed? Good!

Mindfulness Meditation: You might want to set a timer for six minutes. Find a quiet place and a comfortable chair and put your feet firmly on the ground with your posture upright. Turn the timer on once you've gently breathed in and out using the deep belly breathwork described previously. As you do so, pick a spot on the wall. Stare at the site on the wall. Your eyes will get heavy. Just keep looking at the spot. As thoughts arise, please note them and gently see or hear yourself pushing them away as you continue focusing on that spot on the wall. As you gently breathe in and out, think of the sensations you feel in your body. These are only sensations. Continue slowly breathing in and slowly breathing out as you focus on that spot. As more thoughts arise, please note them and imagine yourself pushing them away and out of sight. When the timer goes off, you're done! Fantastic!

You have done your first mindfulness meditation. Over time as you practice more, you can increase your time. However you prefer.

Now let's talk about visualization meditation. Here you'll initially repeat what you learned in the other two meditations. Then you'll visualize an outcome with this one. There are a few examples in the following paragraphs: get yourself ready for each of them in the next section.

Better Self-Esteem: Find yourself a quiet place to relax. Scan your body and release any tension as you take a few deep belly breaths. Find a spot on the wall and concentrate on it. When your eyes get heavy, gently close them. Imagine a colorful light, the color of your choosing, entering your body, usually at the top of your head. Imagine this light is positive, radiant energy. Feel the energy coursing through your body, filling your mind and body with positive self-beliefs. See positive energy flowing throughout your body, making loops and curls and ups and downs, and hear the sound it echoes as this energy reaches every internal part of your body. Then when this energy comes and completes swooshing throughout your feet, visualize all your negative thoughts, tensions, and other junk this energy seized, all gently exiting through your toes and only leaving vivacity behind.

Better Parenting: Imagine this white or colorful light entering your body through the crown of your head and gently opening your mind to all possible things. Today the possibility of being an excellent parental role model and increasing positive connection and engagement with your children is being brought to you by this light. Imagine seeing yourself in that positive role. What would you see? Can you hear your children's positive reactions as they interact with you? What would their facial expressions be? Visualize being with them and take a moment to be there in your heart and mind. Feel how doing so feels. Breathe in this visual, holding that picture close to your heart. Great! Now visualize the light gently leaving your body and taking any negative energy that arose with it. Whish ... With continued meditative breathing, repeat two more times if needed. Then open your eyes and gently breathe in and out.

Increasing Courage: Imagine a light consisting of courageous energy entering your body. As it does so, visualize yourself radiantly standing in front of a large audience. Your energy sensations vibrate with courage. Envision yourself filled with courage. What would that look like for you? How would the audience sound? Imagine being filled with audacious liveliness and notice how that would feel. See that moment, breathe in that moment, and hear yourself be in that moment. Take another deep breath in and out. As the energy leaves your body, see your fearful cells being carried away. See them going, one by one. Watch them leave your body. Take another deep breath in and out. Now open your eyes and gently breathe in and out.

You may repeat each of these without experiencing a break in your trance with your routine and time permitting. Then utilize daily or weekly as you can.

Mark continued addressing his panic attacks with the help of meditation and mindfulness processes tailored to his needs. He learned he could thwart any panic attacks he felt with these methods. My work continued with him until he regained his self-assurance, had mastered these techniques better, and agreed he was ready. His final words were that his life had miraculously changed for the better.

These exercises can increase your quality of life, whether you desire more peace and serenity or a transitional change. Either way, please set aside a few minutes each day, to begin with, for your relaxation meditation or mindfulness practice. Remember to utilize your proper breathwork before meditation or in general. As you gain confidence practicing one of these meditations, please try the other examples.

Work with these to reach the desired outcome you wish to obtain as best you can. Most people report increased relaxation, increased concentration, and decreased stress as a minimum. This book aims to give you tools to improve the quality of your life and be ready to open doors to other possibilities. If you are seeking a transformation beyond the scope of this introduction, please reach out to me. My website is www.cathyherring.com. You can contact me by email or book a free discovery call.

In the next chapter, we'll address some quick and easy applications to help you experience excellent health with your busy routine.

Chapter 8

Nutrition and Daily Activities

Our bodies are marvelous. They're constantly working to defend us from invaders. Your best health is crucial for living your best life. Daily movement and proper nutrition are two key elements essential for your excellent health. Your body is designed to move and help you be at your best. When you supply your body with healthy nutrients and daily movement, like eating fruits and vegetables and walking, your body is likely to feel better and operate at its optimum level. But if neglected by consuming harmful diets and having a lack of beneficial activity, your body will feel out of shape. Over time, your body will feel physically and mentally sluggish and may be at risk for illnesses. It's best to make healthy changes now before you acquire an ailment. Adopting essential nutritional habits and daily movement also contributes to healthy longevity.

Taking proper care of yourself with excellent nutrition and daily activities is not a priority for many American households. This may be true for you, too, regardless of where you live. For instance, when I was growing up, fast food chains and instant box meal preps were up and coming. I grew up with seven brothers and sisters, and money was tight. We rarely ate outside our home except at family gatherings. That meant we ate home-cooked meals made from scratch with no extra unknown ingredients such as artificial preservatives, artificial sweeteners, etc.

For instance, I remember when frozen TV dinners became a big hit. My mom was thrilled to get a break from cooking. One day she bought enough dinners for all of us. That evening, we were excited to try this innovation for modern living. All of us were sitting around the black-and-white TV in our living room. One by one, my mom and the older siblings brought out fresh hot TV dinners for each of us. When we were all served, we began devouring what we thought was an excellent-tasting meal while watching TV. What a treat, we thought. Eating TV dinners while watching TV was a new experience for us.

McDonalds and a few other fast-food places had sprung up too. Once a week, Mom would clean a house for another family member for extra spending money. She'd save it for something special if she didn't need the money to pay for something else. Once or twice a month, on a Friday night, she'd surprise us by bringing home fantastic burgers, fries, and shakes. That era marked the beginning of a significant change in American diets. Fast forward to today when fixing frozen or pre-made foods, getting takeout, and eating out are the primary staples in the American diet. These advancements, along with many others, have lowered the beneficial nutrients in people's diets. Plus, many food sources have introduced higher rates of preservatives, artificial contaminants, and other nonfood items into our food supply, which can be unsafe for people.

Does your diet provide the nutrients your body needs without harmful ingredients? This chapter focuses on giving you some quick and easy tools to apply to help you live a healthier lifestyle, which is another component of igniting the power within you and living a better life. Please read this chapter through to the finish, so you can apply small changes and be on a healthier path overall. This is especially important if your sustainability is primarily prepackaged food, fast food, and sweets with little daily activity. Let's talk about adding better quality food to your diet and daily movement to help you be at your best, especially as you age.

In this book, when I mention "diet," I mean anything you eat and drink daily. I'm not making references to any specific diet. Being interested in and able to take care of your body, mind, and spirit is essential. Hopefully, you will become more interested in healthier eating and daily movement. This chapter intends to provide health education, background information, and advantages for participating in daily activities and increasing your nutritious food intake.

The cracked, blistery-looking palm of Sheila's dominant hand was not healing, even after trying numerous creams, including the one recommended by her dermatologist. Sheila was a real estate agent. She loved her job. But this rash had overcome the palm of her right hand during the last two years, and quite frankly, she was embarrassed. Whenever she met a new client or agent, they inevitably shook hands. Each time Sheila shook their hand with her rash-looking hand, she felt obligated to explain that she didn't have a contagious condition. Then she wondered if they believed her. And so she began wearing a massive Band-Aid over the infected palm so her blistery hand was not as noticeable.

Since her condition was not improving, eventually, her family doctor set up a referral to a dermatologist community in a larger city. Sheila set up an appointment and ventured out with high hopes. The young doctor seemed knowledgeable and interested in Sheila's problem. She examined Sheila's hand and visited with her for quite some time. She concluded Sheila had psoriasis, an autoimmune skin condition.

The doctor recommended prescription medication as the only solution. Sheila was disappointed because she suffered from medication sensitivities most of her life. She no longer sought pharmaceutical medication as an option unless her life depended upon doing so. She felt desperate for relief and thought, *This condition is hindering me. I will try this. Maybe this is the solution.* "The doctor assured me this medication was what I needed for this psoriasis," Sheila reassured herself.

Since her options were limited and she didn't like taking medications for the long term, she was eager to find other solutions for her health. She kept searching for alternative answers and wondered if there was a link between her food intake and this autoimmune disease. She began questioning how she could help her body heal. She pondered how she and her family could be more preventive with their health.

Wanting to know more about preventive health and wellness myself, in October 2019, I hosted an online summit: *Unleash Your Potentials: Discover How Health & Wellness Can Increase Your Confidence & Inner Self-Worth, Improve Relationships, and Live the Life You Love.* I gathered several medical professionals to host a health and wellness summit with twenty outstanding experts from the health field, such as MDs, psychologists, and nutritional and energy coaches. My audience, which might have included some of you, also included Sheila. Together we learned about the importance of living a healthy lifestyle and some simple changes we could implement now.

Even though these experts were interviewed individually, many of them believed there is a correlation between eating certain foods and increasing your chances of acquiring an autoimmune disorder. Others addressed significant links between mental health and poor diets. Some suggested we are experiencing an onslaught of subtle poisoning due to toxic ingredients from pesticides, cleaning products, hair and body products, artificial flavorings and preservatives, and high amounts of sugar added to many products or found in our environment. Several medical experts concluded that improper diets and environmental toxins can contribute to subtle attacks on our bodies.

In the meantime, Sheila got the prescription and looked forward to her hand finally improving, if not going into remission. She wanted to believe this medication would be the miracle cure. Sheila held out hope for the first couple of months, but the condition did not improve. She experienced unpleasant complications by taking the medication. Her quality of life was compromised. She soon lost faith that this medicine would give her the relief she desperately wanted.

Now, did you know there are over one hundred known autoimmune disorders? The NIH states, "In autoimmune diseases, proteins known as autoantibodies target the body's own healthy tissues by mistake, signaling the body to attack them." Furthermore, research has shown these attacks can affect any body part, weakening bodily function and even becoming life-threatening. You may know someone with one of those disorders, if not yourself. Some common ones are lupus, psoriasis, Hashimoto's thyroiditis, celiac disease, MS, and asthma. Several health experts think cancer is an autoimmune disorder. Being healthy helps you live better, thus assisting your body in warding off autoimmune diseases and other compromised health issues.

If you or one of your close family members experience an autoimmune disorder, you know they can be highly concerned. Many autoimmune diseases have debilitating effects, which are costly and time-consuming. The quality of living your life is disrupted. Many health experts claim autoimmune disorders are on the rise. Some health professionals claim research states that each generation will experience more bouts of autoimmune diseases than the previous generation if the course trajectory is not changed. Why is this happening? What can each person do to prevent themselves from getting these disorders if that is a possibility? Some answers are attributed to genetics, but that is not the only answer.

Many of the experts who participated in *Unleash Your Potentials: Discover How Health & Wellness Can Increase Your Confidence & Inner*

Self-Worth, Improve Relationships, and Live the Life You Love 2019 online summit (Herring, [Host] 2019) stress that certain foods, such as organic fruits and vegetables, can aid in maintaining your health. Aging with better health helps ensure you can fully participate in your daily activities, mentally and physically.

Throughout my 2019 summit, the medical community mentioned two key components that help with prevention and combat symptoms. They're worth examining if you'd like to live better.

1. Nutrition (your diet consists of what you eat)

2. Physical movement

Nutrition: Many of the summit's medical professionals believe our bodies constantly strive to be healthy. One way your body maintains that status is by eating proper nutrition—a wide range of food that is more nutrient dense than others. Doing so helps your body develop and maintain healthy cells to do its job—taking care of you. The typical American diet has a high caloric intake with little nutritional value. It also consists of low-fat fresh vegetables and fruits. If you can relate to that, slightly adding more healthy ingredients over time will be a start for you.

To get started, a person can begin adding an extra helping of fresh fruit and vegetables, preferably organic and non-GMO, to their daily meals. If a person is eating processed desserts, attempt to take one away daily or every other day and replace it with a healthier alternative. As people add more nutritional food to their diets, they can acquire a taste for these more nourishing foods. I know that sounds generic, but it can happen. Patience may be warranted. If people don't change their eating habits, their bodies may not be as healthy as they wish. Their bodies can begin to break down sooner than later. What if changing your food choices now prolongs your health so that you can continue your daily activities and live a better quality of life as you age?

Here are some things the experts mentioned. Get involved in what you and your family eat. Read the prepackaged foods and drinks labels. What are the ingredients? Are there words you don't know? You might want to find out what they are and if they are harmful. Many experts agreed to shy away from foods with certain artificial flavorings, preservatives, colorings, especially red dye, and large amounts of sugar. Some health experts think those items are not suitable for maintaining your best health and may contribute to acquiring some auto-immune disorders. You will notice a difference even with tiny changes if you are not eating a healthy diet. You do not need to attempt changing your entire diet overnight if you are not in harm's way. As always, you may need to check in with your health professional before making significant changes.

I'm not a nutritionist, but I have learned quite a bit over the last few decades due to my interests. I can't recommend anything, but I will tell you what I do or what experts have suggested. I still don't always eat healthily, but my diet is significantly more beneficial than six or seven years ago. Here are some things I've changed over the last decade.

I did my best to reduce prepackaged ready-made food and move to healthier alternatives, such as adding fresh organic, non-GMO fruits and vegetables to my meals. Since I hosted my summit, we have eaten even healthier. For breakfast, we primarily eat fruits and nuts—our made-up concoction. My husband and I make a weekly fresh vegetable soup variation for dinner. We only add spices, vegetables, and water to the soup base. Then for more variation, we might add chicken or turkey to a serving. We also have a salad without prepackaged dressing. Much healthier than I used to eat, and I enjoy eating it. Ten years ago, you could not have told me it would be my main dinner dish. We still eat out, and I eat other foods occasionally. Your diet should not permanently restrict you from everything, but if you know something's not suitable for you, eat it in moderation, like every other week and not daily. Please do your research. I am not a trained nutritionist, but my diet changes are significant for living in the US. I am sharing my experience to assist you with a starting point or an idea you may choose to do.

What do you drink? Soda, fancy teas, or energy drinks? If you drink any of those, can you begin to eliminate one per day each month? Again, look at the ingredients. Is there anything with high amounts of sugar or fructose corn syrup? Experts say sugar attacks our cells and is a contributor to cancer. I eliminated soda years ago and replaced it with drinking more water. Many health experts agree your daily water intake is one-third of your weight in ounces. For example, a 150 lb person would take their weight of 150 and divide it by three and get 50. So a 150 lb person would drink 50 ounces of water daily as part of their health regimen. Now take your weight and divide it by 3. What is your number? Does your water intake correlate with the amount you acquire? If not, research and change your intake.

By now, taking the medication was taking Sheila's life away. She was working nine to five. She took a pill once a week on Friday. Then she felt sick all weekend. Even though she was tired, the medication caused her to experience racing thoughts for twenty-four to forty-eight hours. She didn't get much rest. When the medicine wore down, she was exhausted. However, now her weekend was over, and it was time for her to return to work. She'd be tired for the week. This regimen continued for six months.

When Sheila returned for her updated doctor's visit, she asked if there were other solutions. Her doctor didn't give her any other options. Sheila inquired about the laser light; the doctor said that wasn't an option. Sheila explained the medication was not improving her hand's condition. She informed the doctor that the drug was creating more problems for her. The doctor didn't seem to care or offer any other options. Sheila left her doctor's office disappointed.

The following week at work, she wondered if this medicine that failed to improve her condition was worth continuing. By now, she was losing clumps of her hair. This solution did not make any sense to her. She decided she did not need to renew the prescription. She had tried the medication for six months. Her hand was not healing, but her overall health was quickly deteriorating. She discontinued this regimen.

Being able to eat nutritiously is a process. By adding more nutritional food choices to your daily food intake and removing some over time, you may begin to crave healthier options. Then it would help if you continued replacing your poorer choices with healthier ones. Anyone can start this easy task, and you may decide to expand it. After a time, you'll realize doing so isn't as bad as it sounds. I've only spoken about the starting point of changing a poor diet into a healthier one. Please do your research and work with your doctor if need be. Remember, your body is a product of what you consume or don't consume. Make great choices for yourself beginning today!

Physical Movement: Movement is another critical element to maintaining a bright outlook and your health. As John Medina shares in his book *Brain Rules for Aging Well* (2017), "Those who think they have not time for bodily exercise will sooner or later have to find time for illness," by Edward Stanley (Earl of Derby) in 1873.

Research shows that heart attacks are rising since people are less active and sitting more (Medina, 2017). They recommend if you're spending your day sitting, get up every hour and move. John Medina also mentions weekly aerobic exercise, such as a thirty-minute fast-paced walk, increases cognitive functioning in the brain's hippocampus, reasoning, and memory skills. Plus, if you want to help maintain an optimistic outlook, increased physical movement increases your brain's endorphins, elevating your mood.

Most people refer to movement as exercise, but many people have an aversion to the word "exercise." Instead of using the term "exercising" in this book, "exercising" has been replaced with "daily movement" or "daily activities." Hopefully, that sounds more pleasant to you. Is there a physical activity you enjoy that you don't think of as exercising? Some people never consider swimming, bicycling, skateboarding, Pilates, hiking, martial arts, or walking as exercise. They enjoy those activities, and they can be regarded as "exercising." You must keep your body moving, whether walking around your block, jumping jacks in the living room, dancing, running in place, or doing yoga. If this isn't your forte, what daily activity would you enjoy or attempt to enjoy? Maybe you'd prefer to join a group program like rumba, water aerobics, or tai chi. Whatever fits your style. Just keep moving. Thus, nutrition and movement are:

- for keeping your mind sharp
- having a positive attitude
- keeping your body fit and well

Sheila informed a friend of her experiences with her dermatologist. She shared that when she didn't renew her prescription, she received a phone call from the doctor's nurse. The nurse demanded that Sheila renew that prescription immediately when the nurse discovered she was no longer taking the medication. Even though Sheila thought the nurse would be interested in hearing what she had to say, the nurse wasn't. After several demanding orders from the doctor's nurse attempting to get Sheila to renew her medication, Sheila quietly hung up. She was appalled by the nurse's behavior.

Her friend was shocked. She suggested Sheila attempt a gluten-free diet. Sheila liked the idea and slowly began switching gluten-containing products for gluten-free ones. At first, she found changing her diet challenging, but over time she became about 99 percent gluten-free. As she did so, her hand began miraculously improving. With that improvement, Sheila was more motivated to eat more food without gluten and consume more fresh salads, fruits, and vegetables. She claimed that when she was about 80 percent gluten-free, the hand rash was less bothersome and significantly diminished. With that inspiration, Sheila claims she eats healthier now than ever. She watches her intake of sugar-laden foods and keeps her sugar below 50 grams daily. She also attempts to stay away from processed foods. Sheila says her hand condition remains well but occasionally flares up. However, she claimed her diet change improved the quality of her living.

I can't state that a diet change will work similarly for you. Regardless, I'm advocating for you to get more involved, be aware of what you eat, and keep moving for your health's sake. As I stated, become more actively involved if you're not already doing so. If you experience resistance, that's normal. Work through your challenges or reach out to an expert. Sheila didn't want to change her eating habits either. Initially, she began very slowly with minor changes. Now she aims to continue to do so because of her results. She says she occasionally eats unhealthy food and returns to her healthy diet without feeling guilty. You can do the same. You may think you're giving up something, but even if you don't have any health issues, you may find that the long-term benefits outweigh the loss you gave up.

Begin today. Don't overthink any of this. As always, check with your doctor or do your research. Don't make drastic changes quickly unless you follow your doctor's guidelines. You may want to get your family involved or create a dedicated community. Together do research and set goals. Remember, what may work for one, may not work for the other. So be flexible. As you gradually add more healthy foods to your diet and remove some unhealthy items, doing so becomes easier. Think about what daily activity you can begin. If you're busy with kids, for a workout, take them to the park and play with them. Play basketball or throw a football with your children. You could walk during your work breaks or your lunch hour. Again, add these actions to your daily living, and eventually, they will become some of your healthy habits.

Sheila also recognized that harsh chemical soaps or cleaning products contributed to her hand flare-ups. Sheila has added nontoxic products to her daily hygiene. She told me her body felt better than it had in a long time. Proper nutrition has significantly decreased her autoimmune disorder symptoms and kept her off medication. As of this writing, Sheila is pleased with her progress.

You need a foundational healthy nutritional and exercise program for your health's sake. Be aware of all the products you encounter. I advocate for you to take responsibility, do your research, and be proactive in your healthy lifestyle. Remember, this is your life. You are the one in charge of how you care for yourself.

Chapter 9

Recognizing Your Core Values

Your core values and standards provide guidelines for living a life that resonates with your soul-being. Core values are those beliefs and attributes that guide your thinking and behavior. You learn most of these from the people who care for you during childhood. However, as you experience life, you will grow, learn, and change throughout your lifetime, and your core values may shift. Some may take priority over others. Some may compete with each other. Your core values influence your positive or negative experiences. You may need to review and reevaluate your core values, especially after a significant life event.

Since your core values help guide your thoughts and behaviors, you will feel aligned with your inner self when your thoughts and behaviors align with your core values. For example, think about what's most critical to you now. Are your core values being honored or compromised with your interactions with others? Your values help determine your life's direction and your boundaries with others. When your values align with your desires and lifestyle, you experience better harmony. Knowing your most important values and not allowing them to be compromised is vital to being true to yourself.

As you live, you might adopt someone else's values without realizing it. For instance, maybe you and another person have different ideas, so you compromise to reach an agreement. However, one of your essential values was compromised in doing so. At the time, maybe you were unaware of how much that bargain would affect you. If this sounds confusing to you, this chapter's embedded story should help illuminate how a possible issue can develop.

Ranae came to see me because her actions were not helping her reach her end goal. She knew what she wanted but couldn't figure out why she wasn't taking the appropriate measures.

Generally, people form their values within the culture, environment, or family they are raised with. Values define you. They consist of concepts and beliefs that have shaped you into being who you are. They can be sacred, such as spirituality, a means to an end, such as persistence, or have intrinsic worth, such as love. When you review a list of core values, you will realize you hold many of those values. Your top core values are your most important ones. Those may vary because they may depend on your phase of life, area, and what is most important to you during that time. You should understand what matters most to you during different stages of your life and align with your top twenty-five core values.

For example, a person in their twenties and unmarried with no children may value family. Still, family is not necessarily an essential value for them if they do not want to find their partner and begin a family. That value would be more critical for a young couple starting a family. So family as a value is less significant for the person who wants to avoid starting a family and finding a partner. Thus, that value may not be a top priority for them during this phase of their life.

Your most essential core values help you set your boundaries. Boundaries set the standards you live by, and knowing your limitations is necessary for living your best life. Sometimes what you truly value and how you live may need to be more aligned. Even though you may be living a good life, having a misaligned system can interfere with living your best life.

The point of this chapter is to review the importance of knowing what is truly important to you by learning your core values, evaluating them, understanding what areas of your life they serve, keeping those boundaries intact, and learning to gently release those or shift the values that no longer serve you well, as Ranae discovers.

She began babbling and profusely crying as she sat in the recliner in a deep hypnotic state. I suggested she take a moment to visualize herself releasing her pain gently. As she did, I quietly rummaged through what Ranae had claimed brought her to see me today. She was thirty-something and distraught because she reported she was never satisfied with her relationships. She said they would end up going nowhere, and she would eventually end them.

Ranae also said she came to see me because she wanted to attract a healthy life partner to create a special relationship that could lead to a healthy marriage. She claimed she was good at finding excellent dates but had recognized something deep inside her was stopping her from fulfilling her wish. She reported that many pursuers were not an ideal match for her, and others could not make long-term commitments. She thought there might be a connection between her resistance and her results, or rather lack of results. As we explored this concept, I suggested putting her in a discovery state of hypnosis, focusing on this personal issue. She agreed, so here we were.

Her sobbing began calming down. She claimed the pain had disappeared too. As she continued in her relaxed state, I suggested she share with me, of course, with no attached feelings, and in her safe place, what she remembered she saw or felt before the pain overcame her. She nodded her head as if she understood. Then I could see she was searching to formulate her words. "I was betrayed," she stammered.

"Betrayed?" I echoed.

"Yes," she claimed.

"Can you tell me more?" I inquired, reminding her she was now an onlooker and safe in this room.

"Yes, I didn't understand why his mother didn't like me. I liked his family and him, but our relationship was growing apart. We were experiencing difficulties, and we were trying to work through them. Regardless, his mother wanted us to discontinue our high school sweetheart relationship ..." she said as she trailed off for a few minutes.

I interjected to help her get focused again. "So his mother wanted you two to break up?"

"Yes," she began gently sobbing, "that weighed heavy on my mind." She paused as if deep in thought.

"That weighed heavy on your mind," I echoed.

Ranae continued, "I kept thinking I'm not good enough if his mother doesn't want me. I don't need to be in this relationship," she continued. "So I broke up with him and tried to keep my feelings in check. Day after day, he kept attempting to see me. He was heartbroken and expressed his feelings profusely. His perseverance and resistance crushed my heart more than anything. I secretly vowed to myself I would never be in a serious relationship again...." she trailed off. "I never wanted to hurt someone so badly......."

"I see."

She continued. " I was young and didn't know what I was doing."

81

Now, take a moment, breathe in a nice slow deep breath, and slowly release it while you think about your values and virtues. So how can you uncover your most significant twenty-five personal core values? What are they, and what do they consist of?

Here I ask my customers to research what they believe they stand for mentally, such as reviewing all the rules, conduct, and implied rules they were taught through one means or another that they still utilize. As you do this, please take a moment and write them down. Then identify what values you would attach to those rules. Next, write down the value(s) you associate most with that idea.

As you work on the following exercises, please create a folder so you can save these lists and easily find them. Now you can work on the following exercise step by step or all at once. Either way, please save your work so you can continue working when you need to take a break or need to look over it later.

Step 1

What were your rules? Write down any value you assigned to those rules.

Rule: Do well in school. *Education/Cooperation* is important.

Rule: Do my job well. *Productivity/Responsibility* is important.

_____

_____

Now review those values. Are they still true for you? If so, how important do you believe they are to you? For instance, what matters most to you? What has been successful for you, and what have been failures?

Now, with those questions in mind, analyze the values you have uncovered. Those answers will provide clues to some of your critical values. Write notes beside any value you found, such as "Having this one blocks my career progress." Notice fifteen to twenty-five that resonate the most with you if you have uncovered that many. Please see the exercises that follow so that you can provide greater detail.

Step 2 - Begin another list.

Brainstorm

1. Using the list at the end of this chapter as a guideline or others on the Internet, create a *new* list of twenty-five or more values that highly resonate with you.

2. Compare this list to the one you previously created. The ones that are on both lists will be a good indication you are utilizing those. Mark those with a star.

3. Now, review your second list once again. Look at the unmarked values and see how they resonate with you. If you believe strongly in them, mark them with a plus.

4. Now put your star values in one column marked STAR and your plus values in another marked PLUS, and use that list as your CURRENT VALUES WORKING LIST.

Since your marked stars have shown up twice, those are probably the ones you work most with. Let's do a little more research.

Step 3:

Here is another exercise to help you clarify your most essential values currently. Create a worksheet with four columns. Using your current values worksheet list, plug in your star and plus values. Try to narrow down your 'Keep portion' to about 40 most important values, give or take.

Current Values Working List

Value How does this serve me? What area? Keep as Important? Modify?

83

Most people think of values as serving them in all areas of their lives. But what if you looked at each area of your life differently? In his book, *Get Out of Your Mind and into Your Life*, Steven C. Hayes, PhD (2005; pp. 175–176) states that our values are assigned to ten different domains in our lives. These are: *Intimate Relationships; Parenting; Other Family Relations; Friendships/Social Relations; Career/Employment; Education/Training/Personal Growth; Recreation/Leisure; Spirituality; Citizenship; Health/Physical Well-Being.*

Step 4:

Write down these ten domains (or areas of your life) as noted by Steven C. Hayes and assign your values to these domains. Initially, put as many as you think correlate to each domain. You will find some values can be assigned to more than one domain. That is perfectly okay.

5. Now go through each domain and narrow your values down to the five most important values for you in each domain area.

6. In each domain, prioritize your values, with 1 being the most important and 5 being the least important. Keep your list and refer to it if need be.

Congratulations on completing all four steps.

After all that work, these completed four steps help you narrow down your most significant values and in what areas of your life you utilize those values. The last list will help you understand what values you believe are the most critical, uncover what values you use most frequently, and in which areas of your life.

Here are some thoughts to ponder. Remember, this list is a guideline only. Once you uncover those values, think about how they are working for you. Recognize how they guide you. Reflect upon that. Do you believe you are in sync with your beliefs? If so, great. If not, think about what is obstructing you.

Be easy on yourself. Take this seriously, yet not so severely. However, on a cautionary note, if you uncover some unresolved gut-wrenching boundary issues that you are uncomfortable with, please speak with a professional such as a certified trauma-informed or licensed mental health professional. This book is not intended to be a substitute for mental health advice.

What can you adjust so that you are more aligned with what resonates with you? Remember, you can only do the best you can do at that moment in life. Make note of things you dislike and work on adjusting or discarding those actions or qualities. Make note of qualities or actions you do like and work at maintaining or increasing those. Your actions and belief system can be changed, improved, and forgiven over time. *Over time* is key here. Now, please be cautious with this and avoid getting overzealous. This is a *guideline* for you to be aware of to understand yourself better. Remember, you might modify or reprioritize your values as you learn more and experience significant life events.

It would be best if you didn't overthink this and are flexible. The point is to uncover your most important values and whether they are serving you well. This technique helps you find which values serve you best. Then if you are up for more soul-searching, rearrange your results from top priority to least. If you need help, call a trusted friend and talk this out. Often, other people in our lives can offer an objective point of view. People who know you well can probably name some of your highest values and reasons why they believe so.

"Why did I give in? I betrayed myself by not trying," she stated as she began sobbing again. "I realized I have been afraid.... I picked relationships that sucked. I never felt I was good enough."

"I see," I gently stated.

She rested for a few minutes. Soon she was awakened back to her conscious state. We discussed what she had uncovered.

This technique helped Ranae better understand how her values played a significant role in her life. This offered some insight into her values and misaligned actions. She valued being married to a good man and having a family, yet she found herself in compromising relationships. She stated she thought she betrayed her ethics and exclaimed, "Now I know why I would not date worthy men. Jeez, I am now aware, and I must accept this—" She abruptly stopped.

Then I inquired, "What I understand is you believe you do not want to be hurt or hurt others in your dating relationships. Do you believe you are attracting men you will not commit to also?"

"YES," she exclaimed, realizing that scenario resonated with her.

So Ranae uncovered what was amiss and why she had difficulty moving forward positively. Under hypnosis, she had discovered a personal commitment she vowed to keep was no longer serving her. That commitment clashed with what she had always valued. To summarize, when Ranae was younger, she promised to protect herself emotionally which led her to not participate in meaningful relationships for her. Now, as an adult, she recognized her subconscious mental boundaries were harming her, not helping her. It was time to shift what she unconsciously thought was an essential value; This value no longer protected her.

Many people make self-preservation commitments in troubling times to protect themselves. Some people realize just that later in life and course-correct themselves. Others never do, and some seek assistance as Ranae had done.

How about you? As we learn, grow, and change throughout our lifetime, we may discard some, recommit to others, or adjust our needs. If so, do you need to reevaluate your values? You do not need to be perfect. Just allow yourself to have an increased understanding when you uncover some core value and belief mismatches by forgiving yourself and others. Love yourself and others as you are. Remember, living life is a process.

Ranae felt so much better once she understood what was stopping her. She began claiming her life back. She continued her work with me to help guide her to what she truly valued, and I positively supported her journey. She didn't want to take a chance and regress due to old habits calling her back.

Even though you might wish for change, familiarity is challenging to resist sometimes. Ranae got much more robust and courageous. She began joyfully dating the man of her dreams. They were friends first, partners next. Each desired a committed relationship and worked toward achieving that goal as best as possible. At the time of this writing, she is happily married, and they are beginning their family.

Remember, what matters most is understanding how your values or lack of values serve as your life compass. What do you need to do differently to get the lifestyle results you want today and in the future? Be open to change and have hope to do so. Things are constantly changing.

Core Values (not all-inclusive):

Ability	Abundance	Acceptance	Accomplishment
Achievement	Adaptability	Accuracy	Alertness
Altruism	Ambition	Adventure	Affection
Anticipation	Alertness	Appreciation	Approachability
Assertiveness	Attentiveness	Availability	Awareness
Boldness	Balance	Beauty	Bravery
Being-ness	Belongingness	Benevolence	Blissfulness
Bravery	Brilliance	Calmness	Capability
Candor	Caring	Camaraderie	Certainty
Challenge	Cleanliness	Clarity	Commitment
Charity	Chastity	Cheerfulness	Charm
Cleverness	Comfort	Closeness	Cognizance
Compassion	Competence	Complacency	Completion
Confidence	Congruency	Connection	Consciousness
Contentment	Cooperation	Cordiality	Common sense
Concentration	Consistency	Credibility	Conviction

Courage	Creativity	Curiosity	Dependability
Daring	Devotion	Dignity	Decisiveness
Determination	Discretion	Diligence	Desire
Discovery	Dreamfulness	Drive	Diversity
Eagerness	Education	Effectiveness	Efficiency
Expressiveness	Excellence	Exploration	Extravagance
Extroversion	Empower	Energy	Ethical
Famous	Fearless	Ferocious	Fidelity
Focus	Flexibility	Faith	Fame
Fitness	Fortitude	Freedom	Friendship
Frugality	Fun	Generosity	Genuineness
Genius	Giving	Grace	Gratefulness
Greatness	Gregariousness	Growth	Guidance
Happiness	Harmony	Honesty	Health
Humor	Humility	Hope	Honor
Helpfulness	Heroism	Holiness	Hygiene
Imagination	Impeccability	Independence	Insightfulness
Ingenuity	Inquisitiveness	Integrity	Inspiration
Instinctiveness	Introversion	Intuitiveness	Intimacy
Joy	Judiciousness	Justice	Keenness
Kindness	Knowledgeableness	Leadership	Learning
Liberty	Liveliness	Logic	Loyal
Longevity	Love	Majesty	Mastery
Maturity	Meekness	Mellow	Meticulous
Mindfulness	Moderation	Mysteriousness	Modesty
Motivation	Neatness	Nerve	Obedience
Open-mindedness	Optimism	Opulence	Order
Organization	Outrageousness	Originality	Passion
Patience	Performance	Persistence	Playfulness
Potential	Power	Present	Productivity
Professionalism	Prosperity	Purpose	Proficiency
Polish	Preparedness	Pleasure	Practicality
Popularity	Persuasiveness	Precision	Privacy
Prosperity	Prudence	Purity	Qualification
Quickness	Quietness	Realism	Readiness
Reason	Recognition	Recreation	Reflection
Relaxation	Reliability	Resilience	Resourcefulness

Respect	Reverence	Richness	Responsibility
Risk	Rigor	Sacrifice	Satisfaction
Security	Self-control	Selflessness	Self-realization
Self-reliance	Sensitivity	Sensuality	Serenity
Sexuality	Significance	Silence	Silliness
Simplicity	Smart	Sophistication	Sincerity
Skillfulness	Solidarity	Solitude	Soundness
Spirituality	Spontaneity	Stability	Stillness
Strength	Success	Support	Supremacy
Surprise	Savvy	Sympathy	Synergy
Stewardship	Tactfulness	Thankfulness	Thoroughness
Talent	Teamwork	Temperance	Thoughtfulness
Timeliness	Tolerance	Toughness	Traditional
Tranquil	Transparency	Trust	Trustworthy
Truth	Thrifty	Transcendence	Understanding
Unique	Utility	Valor	Vigor
Vitality	Victory	Vision	Virtue
Vivacity	Warmth	Watchful	Wealth
Wholesome	Winning	Wisdom	Wittiness
Wonder	Worthiness	Welcoming	Wonder
Zeal	Zest	Zing	

Chapter 10
Spirituality

Jack was furious, and Nancy looked like she was going to collapse. I motioned with my hand for Nancy to be patient while Jack continued to rage, flapping his arms all around. "I try to be a good father and husband. I love my family! I'm doing the best I can, but it isn't working. She's ready to throw it all away. We're here today because I begged her to come here. I don't want to lose my family, but I don't know what else to do!"

He sighed heavily as he quickly sat down with an angry look written all over his face.

I acknowledged what he shared and reassured him I appreciated his truthfulness. Then I reassured both as a team we would do our best to get to the core of this issue as I continued to evaluate the situation. "I have solutions for you. Please be patient as this assessment continues."

"We are spiritual creatures, (2012, p. 45)" states Leo Booth, *from Spirituality and Recovery: A Classic Introduction to the Difference Between Spirituality and Religion in the Process of Healing: A Guide to Positive*

Living. "You only begin to live when you recognize the spiritual power that has been given." (2012, p. 44)

Spirituality is an essential core value. Personal spirituality is a spiritual journey of connectedness and meaningfulness for creating and maintaining your life's purpose. Being spiritual means living life; you are not an outsider looking in. Spirituality helps you experience clarity, focus, and the opportunity to live an exciting and relevant life. Within the essence of your being is your spirituality. It guides and develops your moral compass. Your health and well-being are also affected by your spirituality.

Purposeful spirituality guidelines intend to keep people from overtly harming themselves or others. For example, many have regulations about not eating or drinking excessively, and not engaging in violence which helps a person be less likely to drink excessively or commit crimes. Thus, practicing spirituality aids one in learning and developing a moral code of conduct. Spiritual people honor others and themselves wisely.

Many who practice spirituality believe there is something outside of themselves that is divine and larger than life, such as God. They believe this spiritual all-being has their best interests at heart. They turn to this almighty being when they need to seek guidance, refuge, solitude, comfort, etc. Some believe practicing spirituality with others, such as belonging to a church or mosque, practicing with a meditation or yoga group, or belonging to self-recovery/development groups such as AA and Al/Anon, is essential and helps grow connections with others. The essence of spirituality encourages one to treat others with kindness, including letting go of resentment and practicing forgiveness. They benefit by experiencing less isolation and developing deeper bonds with the divine and those around them.

Being spiritual helps you feel better physically and mentally and experience less stress. Research has shown that people with a vigorous spiritual life—regardless of their beliefs—live up to 18 percent longer than those who do not practice personal spirituality. Practicing spirituality helps people find purpose and push onward despite hardships when difficult times arise. All these benefits demonstrate why having spirituality is essential. Any journey toward self-improvement needs a belief component that encourages reflection and contemplation.

As I seriously looked Nancy in the eyes, I gently inquired, "I heard what Jack stated, and now please let me know what upsets you. Also, as I said earlier, everything is fair game here; please honestly share your story."

And I quickly glanced at Jack and reminded him to be respectful. He nodded in agreement as Nancy continued the conversation about their conflicts and how Jack did not understand her. As she did so, I was listening to her and watching Jack. *Are both being truthfully honest, and will they work together to sort things out with their fragmented relationship and communication issues?* I could only believe so.

Nancy claimed he doesn't listen to or consider her needs when planning things. However, she remarked, "He used to."

Now with two children, whom they both agree they love dearly, they admitted they are having trouble with their relationship. Neither stated they wanted to give up, but Jack and Nancy didn't know any other solutions. They were weary of the current situation.

What is the difference between spirituality and religion? Religion, by definition, is a collection of beliefs with specific patterns and symbols defining how people are to practice this religion. Religion is an outward expression of your faith journey that provides you guidance and is an expression of your beliefs. Currently, there are thousands of different religions. Each is highly diverse and reflects an entire world of ideas.

However, when you go back to the origins of any religion, you'll find a spiritual component at the core of it. Some faiths, not all, have gotten caught up in their belief system's rules and rote learning. Religion typically already has profound truths written down somewhere, whereas spirituality focuses on discovering the profound truth for yourself. These beliefs are not mutually exclusive. The religious person will want to study these truths to understand how they pertain to their own life—giving them a spiritual journey not dissimilar to the spiritual person.

While there are many more aspects to religion and spirituality, their importance in your life matters, whether you're more comfortable in a religious setting or would prefer to practice your spirituality more personally. You'll find emotional and even physical benefits for both. A spiritual belief system is integral to personal growth and development and improves mental and physical health. So don't be afraid to explore the deeper truths and what they mean to you.

Typically, spirituality is an inward journey process. Someone spiritually seeks a personal connection to understand themselves better. Spirituality encourages inner reflection and is often practiced alone. However, many religions encompass a spiritual component within their content. Either one or both are important for living a better life. This chapter focuses on spirituality since spirituality can be practiced alone or within a religious affiliation.

Jack and Nancy's relationship needed an infusion. After both shared what was on their minds, each seemed more settled. However, their tempers were still flickering. So I brought out two pads of paper and asked each to write down six things they were thankful for about the other or their family. Initially, both are resistant. Neither wanted to give in at first. They just sat there. Then I repeated the directions. I reminded them they were in my office for a reason.

Jack was skeptical because he shared that this strategy could have been a better use of time. "How can our problems be fixed with a sheet of paper?" he exclaimed.

I informed him to get busy. He might be surprised. Nancy took a deep breath, sighed heavily, and began working. Now Jack wasn't going to be left alone. He got busy too.

They began recalling past events and reminiscing. Both seemed to have lost their spiritual path, the glue that brought them together. Living with resentment, righteousness, anger, stubbornness, and stress challenges people's spirituality. *What would be the glue to get them back together?* were my thoughts as they continued to write.

Resentment upsets most people and hurts the one who holds this emotion the tightest. Both were profusely holding on to their righteousness. Each had stated this issue was familiar. I understood that they were no longer resolving problems that began years ago when their children were babies. These parents were pushing matters under the rug since their schedules were tight—the easiest thing for most busy parents to do since they didn't have time to address them. Their spirituality was suffering because of living busy lives and not being available to address their arising issues.

I was eager to hear their thankful lists. Jack sucked in his pride and began first. He started with the simple answers; that he was grateful for their children and their lovely mother, Nancy. Then Jack began to look at Nancy as he spoke to her. Something magical was happening as Jack continued talking while looking into her eyes. Jack spoke from his heart and went deeper and shared even more. He explained why he was thankful for her and the children, and before he could finish, Nancy had massive tears swelling in her eyes. Then Nancy shared similar thoughts that touched Jack's heart. When each finished, I suggested they hold each other's hands and look fondly into each other's eyes without talking, without saying a word. After a few minutes, I asked them how important it was to each of them to resolve this problem among them. Both agreed it was crucial.

After discussing a few more items, I sent each home with a homework assignment before they left that evening. They were to get two journals, one for each of them. They were to write down what actions they thought would bring the marriage back together. Plus, each day, write down one thing they are thankful for regarding their spouse. Yes, this may sound cheesy to some, but getting back to the fundamentals and finding their spiritual path again is what their rocky relationship needs.

How can we begin again when we lack a spiritual path or lose our way? Begin slowly and honor what practicing spirituality means to you. Do some research. The more you learn, the more you discover your spiritual aspect's importance. You can find spirituality within your religious affiliation or church community. Sometimes people find spirituality in solitude, and other times people see it while helping others. Spirituality is not tangible; it is a sense, an awareness, and an inner knowing.

The spiritual journey doesn't have a destination. You are not looking for an end; you are looking for a way of life. Some questions to ask yourself as you embark upon this journey or reevaluate your path are:

- How can you be productive and live in harmony?

- How can you be responsible and loving?

- How can you treat others with kindness?

- How do you find peace and contentment knowing the journey is ever-changing?

Those are a few questions you might ask yourself when contemplating a spiritual journey.

Then commit to practicing spirituality. Be sure not to take yourself so seriously and laugh at life's absurdities, and things that unexpectantly appear on your path. Follow your flow, and as you do so, begin looking for like-minded people. You may discover your ideal people within religious affiliations, like-minded people with similar interests, or both. Also, search for important teachers and mentors who are honest, trustworthy, and have integrity. They may be someone in your religious community. Set boundaries and use caution when evaluating people so you are following the right crowd. In the meantime, you might enjoy meditation, prayer, and reflection to find inner peace. Affirmations may also help guide you.

Observe things as if you were an outsider looking in. The appropriate spiritual path will appear as you continue researching and moving forward. Be cautious about vexations to the spirit. You do not want to be led astray. Take note of what activities feel rewarding and how they help your self-discovery and personal improvement journey. People experience more clarity and joy, seem more grounded, and better understand why things are happening in their lives. You will notice that the world brings itself together and creates a bigger picture. With spirituality, your life can lead you in a focused direction, and you will understand aspects of the bigger picture. This knowledge will help direct your steps forward so that you can be successful.

The following week when Jack and Nancy came to see me, they seemed anxious and excited at the same time. *Hmmm*, I wondered if they had made headway. We discussed how their week progressed. They both seemed reassured and more confident. As they read their lists one at a time aloud to each other, there were some remarkable similarities. Both expressed a need for a recommitted partnership and wanted to rekindle the fire. They said they needed to find a new church community because they had quit attending their other church. Each stated they needed personal time and would like to add dating time. Each also agreed family was vital. They realized they needed to forgive each other for the rocky road they had been riding. They claimed they were not ready to give up.

As I watched them interact with each other and convey their thoughts and ideas, express their apologies, thankfulness, and desires to bring their relationship back together, I realized that I was witnessing a miracle. Last week these two were getting a divorce, and this week they were committed to recommitting and making their marriage work. I realized I was the blessed one at that moment. I was almost crying tears of joy with them.

However, this was just a new beginning for them. They proved to one another that they were ready and willing to work to improve their marriage. They had many unfolding tasks in front of them to build a stronger relationship and reunite them. Their thoughts, actions, and behaviors must be reviewed and rebuilt. Some perceptions needed stronger boundaries, along with room for growth and expansion. The process of all those beginnings and endings, ups and downs, discarding and remaking in this journey is part of their spiritual process of being together.

Think about yourself. You may need to change direction occasionally, reevaluate what aligns with you, have your loved ones express what aligns with them, compromise as best as you can, be kind, and allow others to be themselves, too. True spirituality will help you be the best version of yourself.

Chapter 11

Putting It All Together

Successful people's mindsets prepare them for success. Some people have a natural talent for this. Others have learned and cultivated that mindset. All have certain concepts that give them the ability to be winners.

Your success is independent of how big or small your endeavor is. What matters most is that your undertaking aligns with your values, lifestyle, and mindset to operate at your best.

Everybody experiences challenges in their lifetimes. The better you navigate these challenges, the more successful you are at living your life. This book introduced you to several concepts that will assist you with increased awareness, clarity, confidence, inner peace, and strength, helping you navigate life's challenges to move successfully through life. As I stated in Chapter 1, "Living life successfully is a lifelong process."

The concepts assist you with becoming more acquainted with your values and mindset. The first four concepts are action steps primarily to strengthen your emotional resilience. The last three concepts mainly focus on improving physical, clarity, and spiritual health. Each applied idea is like a puzzle piece with its own unique contribution to improving and maintaining your well-being. Together they focus on your mind, physical, and spiritual health. As you work with these puzzle pieces, you create your unique building blocks constructing a solid foundation for living your life. Consistently apply one or two of these notions to begin living a better life today.

Robbie was a friendly, ambitious, and career-driven lady. Robbie was a community leader who had a contagious vivacious vibe. She exuberated confidence as she pursued what she needed and seemed to pursue those issues without a care. Robbie had raised her children, and they had families of her own. She never remarried after her terrible divorce from her husband, and her friends said she never talked about it. Robbie was an older lady who was still making plans and dreaming. She was always well-dressed and kept herself physically fit. Everything looked perfect from an outsider's viewpoint.

A few years ago, I met online with a women's group I was hosting. These women were smart, savvy, and intelligent businesswomen. The COVID-19 pandemic was causing an underlying fear among many people, especially those aged fifty and over. People around the globe were dying from contracting COVID-19. Social distancing was a must, even sometimes around their loved ones. In the USA, many states were locked down. People were shocked and confused. How did this become our "new normal?" Thus, anybody feeling uneasy during this chaotic time seemed understandable.

During one meeting, I explained the difference between irrational and rational beliefs, with several examples of common irrational ones written on my whiteboard. As these ladies were reading and reviewing the negative statements on my board, I noticed some looked troubled. "Remember," I said, attempting to reassure them, "we all have these beliefs from time to time.

99

This is normal. You may wonder if things will ever change when they pop up. Will you be free from these ruminating self-derogatory beliefs?" I continued. "Sometimes, they are still buried underneath. You may not realize that. Also, what you might not have dealt with in years can suddenly appear during stressful times, like the one we are currently living in."

How about you? Do you ever deal with annoying self-defeating statements from time to time?

We can address these by stopping these thoughts and putting out the flame. I continued with an encouraging smile. "That's why you all are here. We have each other and me to get through these opposing challenges." As I looked at the members, most looked tired and discouraged. I thought to myself, *Hmmm, they need to talk.*

I sat down and shared these words with them. "Ladies, your courage, curiosity, and wisdom brought you here today. I have only known you briefly, but I see that and much more in each of you. Since this is an interactive meeting, let's get some feedback. What are some of you thinking and experiencing?" I asked.

A few spoke up. Many shared the same theme. They seemed to be experiencing more negative thinking and worries during this pandemic. Reading the self-defeating statements I put on the board, reminded them of the hopelessness some said. I acknowledged their perspectives.

With that message, the meeting took a different direction. I encouraged every lady to share. One by one, they shared similar problems and stories of distressing experiences that many of them had gone through. Everyone was overwhelmed and frustrated with the situation. They claimed they didn't comprehend why so many negative things were happening simultaneously. I nodded in agreement with them and wondered what I could do differently. I had envisioned this outcome of this meeting differently than this.

As they went around and shared, everyone was supportive of each other. They validated each other's concerns. The connection created by the power of this group soothed everyone's emotional pain as they supported each other. We were all amazed and grateful. At that moment, I added a calming, mindful meditation. They were guided through a deeply relaxing meditation that contained many positive affirmations. These affirmations provided more empowerment in loving themselves, being courageous, having clarity, giving joy and laughter, connecting with others, and staying in touch with supportive people.

The ladies seemed more relaxed and hopeful when we finished. They complimented the meditation and shared their support. Great, I thought to myself. We can resume this group. I shared with the ladies that we needed to regroup stronger and build their resilience during these challenging times. They were nodding their heads in agreement.

After their break, I asked each to return with paper and a pen. When they returned, the topic addressed some of the cornerstone foundation basics. We worked with a thankful attitude by developing a thankful list and each sharing around the room. It didn't matter how unique, minor, or significant the content was. The ladies were empowered by participating. As they shared their messages around the room, the energy became more vibrant as they heard everyone's blessings. They each developed a positive personal affirmation unique to them. I suggested they state that affirmation every day throughout the day until the next group session. Then we concluded.

The next day, Robbie from the group reached out to me to visit. We met for a video chat. After some formal introductions, Robbie confessed she felt like an imposter. Inquiring more, she claimed she put on a façade daily and wasn't the person most people knew her to be.

"Oh really," I curiously emphasized, "please tell me more."

After she did so, I inquired if she always felt like this or if this belief was new. She paused and pondered for a bit. Finally, she said she used to feel that way. After divorcing her husband, she felt anxious and worried and wondered who she was.

"Okay, then what happened?"

She looked at me. "I don't know. One day it seemed as if everything was okay. I got my confidence back, and my happiness and vitality returned. However, since this pandemic began, I feel apprehensive again and unsure. I question myself, 'What if this doesn't work, or I can't do it?' I don't know why I'm doing this. Then I joined your group for reassurance and to move forward. I am struggling. I am struggling," she repeated. "I'm not too fond of feeling like this. What can I do?"

Wow, I thought to myself. I was taken aback. You never know what someone is going through. I maintained my composure and asked her a few more questions. Then I gave her a few options that she could attempt. She thought about those options and decided to stay in the group. She liked the company, she claimed.

She said, "I try to meet up occasionally with my friends and family, but most of it is online. I feel lonely too, and I don't think that is helping either."

I acknowledged.

"However," she continued, "I am ready to get back to myself. May I work privately with you, also?"

I said, "Yes, of course, you got it. Are you ready?"

"Yes," she said.

"Let's begin with some homework to strengthen your resilience."

What did I assign Robbie? She was to start the Attitude of Gratitude assignment and add thirty minutes of aerobic exercise daily to her regimen. She seemed receptive and agreed she could do that.

As I stated earlier in this book, any adult can utilize these concepts, including those who never seem to have any issues. Unexpected challenges arise in life, and successful, happy people understand that. They also have positive strategies to help them face their challenges best. I have presented some plans for you, too, in this book. Remember to use these strategies to keep you more mentally, physically, and spiritually fit during rough times. Doing so helps you bounce back quicker and fight off negativism, so you can be your best.

People also need healthy relationships, connection, engagement with others, laughter, and fun. Keep in touch with your circle of supportive people, and have fun getting together or even just talking when you can. We are social creatures. Hanging out with other people does us well.

The following week when I met with Robbie, I could see a change. She was energetic and more excited than I had noticed before. She reported she was doing her homework. She claimed she needed direction and felt like she was getting it. Exercising improved her outlook again, plus she agreed she needed to do more activity. She claimed she was experiencing more clarity and zest. She was amazed at how alternating two minor changes contributed to experiencing a massive transition in one week.

Robbie was ready for the change. Every time I saw her, usually two times a month, she eagerly accepted her assignments and pursued her endeavors. She diligently did her homework and was very engaged in our meetings. She admitted she was pleased with her positive changes. Robbie understood what she needed to work on and would follow through each time, seemingly taking each concept to heart.

Robbie was able to make good strides by doing the assignments with little resistance. Coaching her was such a pleasure. I was happy for her, like I am for all the clients making positive strides. Robbie demonstrated that diligently applying the techniques with consistency resulted in excellent results for her. She accomplished what she set out to gain and her trials and results demonstrated how living life is progress. Remember everyone's journey is different. If you experience resistance, that's fine too. Keep moving forward.

The ladies' group did well too. They worked diligently on their assignments. Almost everybody was there each week. They seemed more engaged with the sharing around the room and the group's support. Some made friends with each other. They had much success.

In all my years of working with people, some have stood out more than others. I want to say I positively impacted everyone who worked with me, but that would be lying. Sometimes the timing or personalities need to match up. Other times people need to apply themselves more consistently. I enjoy helping others and am delighted when I get students who are ready for changes. You get out of this what you put into this. There is an old saying, "The teacher appears when the student is ready." I hope this book is the teacher you need. If you want more information about what I offer, please get in touch with me at https://cathyherringcom. I would be thrilled to hear from you.

Chapter 12

It Is Time to be Successful

When you picked up this book, you were curious about improving your life and even being more successful. You were interested in how you could be more joyous, happy, and prosperous. You wanted to climb out of experiencing self-doubt and fear and be courageous. You wanted more, but you felt like everything was holding you back.

Whenever you accomplished a new challenge, it felt like another one popped up. You wondered how you could reach your goals after rewriting similar ones year after year and never achieving any. You thought about your dreams and desires and wanted to know if they could become real. Then you found this book. This book reveals simple strategies for attaining your goals and improving your life.

Each chapter brought you easy step-by-step methods for everyday life solutions. As you turned the pages, you witnessed people opening new doors to possibilities. Each chapter's idea ventured deeper with relatable successful stories for you. You learned many people were obtaining positive changes after applying a few solutions. You saw that somebody could quickly implement these methods without interfering too much with their life's routine. Many claim that doing so brought them clarity, happiness, confidence, joy, courage, and the ability to work through their challenges. You realize that adopting these solutions can shift your perspective, strengthen your resilience, and create the belief that you can accomplish what you set out to accomplish. You now have proof that things can change for the better.

Remember Maude from Chapter 2? She was having a difficult time. Not all people will have as much difficulty as Maude, but if she can prosper, why not you? I'm delighted to report I heard from her recently. She told me she had transformed her life. She claimed she is more aligned with her authentic self. Maude said she is happier, more confident, and believes in herself now.

What about Maureen? She also believed, forgave herself, and turned her life around. She found a successful career, raised her children, and married. She admits this is the life she deserves. She stated she needed to learn how to achieve this after making many mistakes along the way.

Remember Mark? He used meditation and mindfulness techniques to overcome panic attacks and keep his job. These stories are just a handful of examples. There are plenty of more powerful results as people put these concepts into use. Are you ready to better your life and be successful too?

It's time for you to apply these solutions. Which ones resonated the most with you? That would be an excellent starting place. Begin putting one or two concepts into action today. You could manifest a new perspective and a healthier attitude in just a few days. You may feel more confident, happy, and adventurous. Add another action if that action doesn't give you the desired results.

Sometimes these actions take longer than expected. You may need to break down your goal into smaller pieces so that you can see your results bit by bit. If you have not done much activity before reading this book, add some movement, such as walking, to your regimen today. Increasing your daily activities can increase your endorphins which can improve your outlook. Adding healthier food to your diet can help improve your health and help you feel better. Practicing mindfulness and meditation can help you improve focus, attitude, and joy! Knowing what you stand for is essential, which can be realized by applying the core value exercise. Practicing spirituality in all you do brings out the best in you.

Another client, LaShonda, came to me seeking relief from her agonizing despair. She claimed she got by, but she wanted more. She stated that she felt trapped. She did not know how to escape her situation, and someone recommended me to her.

Okay, after we examined her situation further, I said, "Let's begin anew."

I talked about how she can change her reality by changing her mindset. "Let's start with a mindful meditation for relaxation and refocus."

She perked up a little and said she would try anything.

We addressed deep breathing and then worked on a mindful meditation like the one in this book. LaShonda relaxed from head to toe generating a radiant smile afterward.

Then I inquired what she is thankful for in her life. As she was naming a few things, I gave her a piece of paper to write them down. She did. When the session ended, I sent her away with a homework assignment. She was to write several things she was thankful for every evening and take a moment to reflect. Each morning, she was instructed to reread what she stated the night before and take a moment to reflect. Then set three intentions for the day. She agreed she could do that.

This book offers many solutions to improve your life quickly and over time. You can apply the methods at your own pace. During

LaShonda's journey of self-discovery, she began with mindfulness meditation in my office, writing her gratitude list every evening and setting daily intentions each morning. Next, we added positive affirmations. She was initially given some simple ones, such as "I am worthy and confident." We always began the session with a mindfulness meditation each week we met up. I noticed LaShonda became happier and seemed more energetic. She reported she was seeing small positive changes in her life already.

As we continued to see improvement, her sessions became monthly. Over the next twelve months, we continued addressing the things in this book. We covered healthy nutrition and daily activities. As she worked on her core values, she claimed she was setting better boundaries with others. Doors were opening for new opportunities. She discovered her spirituality again. Her foundation was growing stronger every month. LaShonda began practicing her meditations at home, too. We worked on increasing her self-talk into more positive statements. She was an excellent student and did well. She even found better paying and more satisfying work during that time. After a year, she was a changed person. She was more confident, happier, focused, courageous, and spiritual with vital resources. She has acquired robust foundational tools, which she pivots her life around. LaShonda claims she has been driven to more success.

You can be just as successful as any of the examples I have shown. You have everything you need to take a positive and proactive approach to live your life successfully by adding new resources to your toolbox and implementing them. Can you imagine the possibilities? As you read through the pages, did you imagine what your life would be like when you are successful? Thinking about your finances, health, family, and spirituality, what did you imagine would change? If you need to, write your thoughts down. Do your thoughts and ideas resonate with you? Does this sound like something you want? Review the concepts.

If you have not already, begin with one action today. Most people can easily apply to be thankful and to state positive affirmations aloud. The most important thing is to start so you can witness the changes. Then as the transformation begins, your perspective will shift, and you will be ready for something that better aligns with you. These actions are just the beginning of a fantastic transformation. Remember, I asked you to *imagine your success*; work toward that. It would be best if you were *ready*, *act*, and *go* for living your new life now.

In closing, here are a few affirmations and mottos to get you started on your new adventure. Remember, "If nothing changes, nothing changes."

"All things happen for a reason."

To increase your self-esteem and confidence:

"I radiate with confidence."

"I live joyously."

"I am happy."

"It is okay to be me."

"I am resilient."

To conquer fear:

"I am courageous."

"Do it anyway."

"Trust God."

"I believe."

"I achieve what I believe."

And lastly, "I am ready!"

And the list is endless.

May you be motivated and inspired to act to better your life beginning now!

For more information about Cathy Herring and any of her upcoming workshops, training, retreats, or other current news, please visit her website at www.mindshiftforsuccess.com or www.cathyherring.com Please sign up to receive your free inspiring e-book and join her fabulous email list where you receive heart-warming affirmations to keep you inspired.

References

Booth, L. (2012). *Spirituality and Recovery: A Classic Introduction to the Difference Between Spirituality and Religion in the Process of Healing: A Guide to Positive Living.* (4th ed.). Health Communications, Inc.

Byrne, R. (2006). *The Secret.* Beyond Words Publishing.

Gandhi, M. (n.d.). AZQuotes.com. Retrieved March 13, 2023, from AZQuotes.com https://www.azquotes.com/quote/353175

Hay, L. (1995) *You Can Heal Your Life.* (2nd Edition). Hay House Inc.

Hay, L. L., Tomchin, L. C., & Olmos, D. (1997). *The Power is Within You* (14th ed.). Hay House Inc.

Hayes, S. C., PhD., & Smith, S. (2005). *Get Out of Your Mind & Into Your Life: The New Acceptance & Commitment Therapy.* New Harbinger Publications, Inc.

Herring, C. (Host) "Unleash Your Potentials: Discover How Health & Wellness Can Increase Your Confidence & Inner Self-Worth, Improve Relationships, and Live the Life You Love." 2019 Vimeo.com 20 October 2019

Hill, N. (2007). *Think and Grow Rich.* Wilder Publications.

Medina, J. (2017). *Brain Rules for Aging Well: 10 Principles for Staying Vital, Happy, and Sharp.* Pear Press.

New American Standard Bible. (1973). Student Edition. (Lockman Foundation). *A.J. Holman Company.*

NIH. Autoimmune Disorders retrieved March 15, 2023 from
nih.gov https://www.niams.nih.gov/health-
topics/autoimmune-diseases

Nongard, R. K., PhD. (2010). *Medical Meditation: How to
Reduce Pain, Decrease Complications and Recover
Faster from Surgery, Disease and Illness.* Peachtree
Professional Education, Inc.

Nongard, R. K. (2012). *Big Book of Hypnosis Scripts: How
to Create Lasting Change Using Contextual
Hypnotherapy, Mindfulness Meditation and Hypnotic
Phenomena.* Peachtree Professional Education, Inc.

Nongard, R. K. (2011). *Magic Words in Hypnosis: The
Sourcebook of Hypnosis Patter and Scripts and How
to Overcome Hypnotic Difficulties.* (2nd ed.).
Peachtree Professional Education, Inc.

Nongard, R., PhD. (2019) *The Seven Most Effective Methods
of Self-Hypnosis: How to Create Rapid Change in
Your Health, Wealth, and Habits.* Independently
published.

Peale, N. V. (1987). *You Can if You Think You Can.* (2nd
ed.). Prentice Hall.

Peale, N. V. (1991). *Power of the Plus Factor* (7th ed.).
Random House Inc.

Peale, N. V. (1982). *Dynamic Imaging: The Powerful Way to
Change Your Life.* Fleming H. Revell Company.

Schultz, J. (2023). 5 differences between mindfulness and
meditation. *Positive Psychology.*

Slogans. (n.d.) retrieved March 15, 2023, from
YourDictionary.com:
https://www.yourdictionary.com/slogan